Sacred

Land

About the Author

Clea Danaan lives near Denver, Colorado, with her husband and daughter. She is a Reiki Master and sound healer, and has studied at Naropa University and the University of Creation Spirituality. Clea has been gardening organically for over fifteen years, from the soggy Pacific Northwest to the arid Rocky Mountains.

Sacred Land

Intuitive Gardening for Personal, Political & Environmental Change

Clea Danaan

Llewellyn Publications · Woodbury, Minnesota

FIRST EDITION
First Printing, 2007

Book design by Rebecca Zins
Cover design by Gavin Dayton Duffy
Cover illustration © Lydia Hess
Interior illustrations © Dover Publications, from *Old-Fashioned Floral Designs CD-ROM and Book* (1990, 1999)

Llewellyn is a registered trademark of Llewellyn Worldwide, Ltd.

The Cataloging-in-Publication Data for *Sacred Land* is on file at the Library of Congress.
ISBN-13: 978-0-7387-1146-1
ISBN-10: 0-7387-1146-2

Llewellyn Publications
A Division of Llewellyn Worldwide, Ltd.
2143 Wooddale Drive, Dept. 0-7387-1146-2
Woodbury, MN 55125-2989, U.S.A.
WWW.LLEWELLYN.COM

Printed in the United States of America
on recycled paper, 50% post-consumer waste

Contents

Chapter 1: *Earth* • 1

Chapter 2: *Air* • 57

Chapter 3: *Fire* • 117

Chapter 4: *Water • 179*

INTRODUCTION

"The environmental crisis is
also our spiritual catharsis.
In healing the Earth,
we heal ourselves."

Kenny Ausubel,
Restoring the Earth

GODDESS

Gaia

THE SUPREME MOTHER Goddess of the Greeks, Gaia birthed the first race of gods and the humans. Her name comes from the Greek word for land, *ge* or *ga*. The people worshiped her at the temples of Delphi, throwing barley and laurel into her sacred cauldron. An omnipotent prophetess, Gaia spoke through the oracle at Delphi, giving advice on matters of home, law, and the land. In Roman mythology, she is called Tellus or Terra.

Gaia is the soul of planet Earth. Her gentle yet all-powerful strength gives life to all green and growing beings and holds us in a protective embrace. She is the whole of the earth, however, and does not regard humans as more important than nature. In our foolish arrogance we have upset the natural balance, and Gaia is working to set things right with the earth changes we face today.

Give thanks to her each day as you enter your garden, and attune with her essence as you work and play with the sacred land. Gaia rules over fertility, motherhood, healing, and dreams, so we gardening sisters can call on her in all we do.

The Healing Garden

In a garden or a forest, roots grow together to form a complex network, a web that shares nutrients, water, and structural support. Arthropods, earthworms, and bacteria live among the lacing of roots, which cradles stones, sustains fungi, and wraps around bones left behind.

We who walk on the surface of the earth rarely see this dynamic labyrinth, but we are a part of it. We are a part of the flow of water as it slips up trees and whispers into the sky, as it falls on the soil and returns to the sea. We too are a part of the burn and glory of sunlight, which sparks all life on Earth. We are a part of the One Breath. We are the gardeners, the stewards of the land.

This book is that interdependent web made manifest in words. It is a guide to the temple of the sacred land that we gardeners tend, with whom we co-create a sacred life. Wander down the paths of these pages as you would a temple garden, peeking between branches or peering into ponds to discover secret nooks and moments of blessing. Take away what you find and share it with others, extending the web further.

Whether you have gardened for years or have only dreamed of planting your first tomato in a patio pot, you will find inspiration in the stories of fellow gardening sisters, the mythology of the world's goddesses, and suggestions for successful gardening.

Throughout this book I will offer meditations to expand your awareness of the energies and beings of the sacred land. Meditation is a time to slip into a changed level of consciousness, a new or different awareness of life and the universe than how we usually operate while moving through our daily lives. Intuitive gardening relies on altered awareness of the land, animals, plants, and elements with whom you garden. You are one part of a great dance, a great holon of birth, regeneration, death, and rebirth. To participate more consciously in this dance of wholeness, you must slow down, tune into your senses (including your psychic sense), and open to the powers that be in the garden.

I write for women who are rediscovering the power of the sacred feminine in their lives, and who want to use that power to create positive change in the world.

I am going to take you along a winding path, introducing you to a garden goddess, then offering information about an aspect of the garden, then taking a pause for reflection. I include information on goddesses to inspire your spirit, to awaken the power of myth. Goddesses and gods grew from people's relationship with their homes, with the wind and water, gardens and forests. By studying deities from around the world, you will understand a bit more about place and about relationship with the sacred land.

I will also introduce you to women making a difference in the world through the sacred garden. They are activists, farmers, artists, and healers who inspire by illustrating how we can make a difference despite seemingly terrible odds. Like these women, you can use your power as a woman of the Earth to heal humanity's broken relationship with the land.

When you think of activism, protest marches or checks sent to nonprofits may come to mind. However, there is another branch of the activism tree, one that grows a little slower but perhaps a little stronger. Engaged stewardship of the land through organic, intuitive gardening slowly but deeply affects our world, from the soil beneath our feet to our children's view of what is sacred to the health of our communities, human and nonhuman. As you heal the land, you heal yourself.

You tend three gardens with this book: in your back yard, in your spirit, and in the world. They are interconnected. At times I will focus on a gardening how-to, like creating compost or incorporating planetary energy in the garden. Other threads include the wisdom of garden allies, from fairies to frogs. At the end of each chapter is a section on taking action in the garden and in the world. We are all woven together like the roots of the trees, and what we do affects others. Just as the roots of your garden do not end at your garden gate, neither does your work as a gardener. The garden can be a powerful tool for personal, political, and environmental change.

This book is a beginning place, a launching point for your own sacred work. You may be inspired to seek out other sources to learn more about how to garden and to learn more about goddesses and ecological activism.

I encourage you to keep a journal as you read, recording your thoughts, dreams, discoveries, and the stories of your garden. Include drawings, poems, rituals, and anything else that speaks of your own journey as a sister of the Earth.

As lighting a candle begins a sacred ritual, I hope my words will help you spark a new relationship with the land—that you will gain a new approach to gardening, and begin to see and know the interconnections among all things. That you will share the love and wisdom of the garden with others as you see the immense power a simple garden has to create personal and planetary change.

We are here on Earth to learn to love. In the garden we visit love again and again, whether that be love for a squash blossom, a child covered in dirt, a community working together, or a miraculous Mother Earth.

May these words help you find love for the garden, yourself, and the planet. May they inspire you to walk your sacred path. I look forward to spending time with you in the sacred land of the garden.

CHAPTER 1

Earth

it's the dark of the earth

where we bury our bones

it's the blessing of the flesh

the child of spirit & stone

it's the only place

we can all agree is our home

it's the dark of the earth ...

Tony Edelblute,
"No Name Thing"

The Sacred Soil

The soil is a vast kingdom beneath our feet, home to giant and minute earthworms, billions of bacteria and micro-organisms, spiders and ants, and wise, ancient stones. Rich black, sandy red, or pale and gritty, it is in the soil that life on land begins. But not all soil is the same—far from it.

The first step to getting to know a garden is to meet and appreciate the soil. The health of a garden depends on its soil. Just as a good house needs a strong foundation or a healthy child needs a stable home, a garden needs well-balanced, healthy soil.

Soil is a garden's immune system. Since soil builds a garden, and the garden brings health and healing to the gardener and the land, we begin our magic-making and world-healing in the dirt.

A few summers ago, I prepared a garden bed that had not been touched for years, a plot of mostly hard-packed clay. I turned over piles of the dark, slate-gray soil with my shovel. The sandy clay, granular but compact and moist, supported a few worms, including two behemoth night crawlers. Bits of charred wood and carbon specked the soil, perhaps remnants of an old burn. It smelled like a dripping cave, damp and cool. I felt a sense of the soil awakening, seeing sunlight for the first time in many years. I also sensed a curiosity from the soil itself and a willingness to explore the co-creative journey of garden-making.

In another bed in another garden, I met very different soil. Pale and gritty, the land had baked beneath Colorado sun for years. Digging it was like scraping ice, hard and unyielding. I felt a mistrust from it, like a rattlesnake eyeing me askance. Beneath this top dry layer lay clay, stone, and bedrock, layers that would give my garden a hardy, determined energy.

Whether you have worked a garden space for years or you approach a new bed that you have never met, take time to get to know the energy, personality, and style of the land. This is the beginning of any sacred gardening partnership.

Getting to Know the Soil

In this book, I offer meditations for getting to know the garden better, and for sinking more deeply into yourself. We begin with the soil, the literal and energetic ground of the garden.

Find somewhere you can touch soil—a comfortable place outside or with a potted plant indoors. Sit in front of your plot of earth, and place your hands gently on the dirt. Feel its temperature and texture. Scoop up a handful, and look carefully at the soil, perhaps with a magnifying glass. Smell the soil.

As you interact with this earth, ask yourself how it relates to your own body. How do you express the qualities of strength and groundedness or of creativity and fertility in your life? Ask the soil aloud or in your mind what it has to teach you about being solid, about growing muscular roots. Feel any shifts in your body as you respond to the soil and it responds to you. When everyday mind-chatter slips in again, let it go, and bring your awareness back to your body and the soil. Take a few moments to still your mind and just be with the soil.

Expand your awareness of soil to include your entire garden, be it acreage or a window box. Walk through your garden, picking up handfuls of soil and extending all your senses. What do you notice? What does the land tell you about its history? How does each area interact with water or sunlight differently? How does the soil smell? Keep checking in with the sensations in your body. How does your heart respond to the soil? Your hands? Your breath, your muscles, your mood?

Open-minded, open-hearted observation is the first step in working with any garden space. Each garden is unique, with its own personality, needs, and quirks. Just as you would in meeting any new friend, spend time listening and looking to know the land on its own terms.

You may wish to start a gardening journal, where you record your journey as a sacred gardener. Begin now by writing down what you discover about the soil. Add to your journal frequently, including drawings, photographs, and observations that are both objective and subjective. All of this information will aid you in working with your garden; testing the soil and feeling it with your heart are simply different ways of listening to the earth. Let your journal and your relationship with the land and its parts evolve like a poem written over time.

Draw a map of your garden in your journal, indicating what you discover from and about your soil, including sense impressions and soil tests. Record different colors of soil, size of the particles, water retention, and other observations. Which areas of the garden are in shade, and which are baked by sun? How does this change throughout the year? From which way does the wind blow in the summer? The winter? Do power lines cross the garden? Is there a nearby source of water? Does a neighboring tree drop leaves, needles, or fruit on your yard? What other elements affect your garden? Include the date of your observations, just to see how your skill of observation using all of your senses, including your "extra" senses, develops and changes over time.

You can also get to know your soil on a more "scientific" level by observing what types of soil make up your land, including its components, pH, and nutrient levels. This is valuable information in co-creating a garden with your land. What you discover about levels of nutrients can confirm what you sense in your body and can provide important information about the land.

GODDESS

Demeter

THE GREAT MOTHER of soil and grain, Demeter gave seeds to the first people and taught them to farm the land. The Doorway of the Mysterious Feminine, she guides us past the garden gate into the sacred womb of life and death. Old myths present her as the trinity of maiden, mother, and crone; originally Pluto was not a god, but a version of the Mother, the chthonic goddess of earthly death (perhaps our recent demotion of Pluto to a dwarf planet marks a resurgence of the power of the Mother). Though more recent tales have split Pluto into Persephone the maiden, Demeter the mother, and Pluto the Underworld god, the ancient world saw these as different aspects of the Great Mother.[1] When we listen to these older myths, Demeter is earth mother of life, death, fertility, and growth.

Say a prayer of thanks to Demeter as you till the soil and plant your seeds. Honor her in the fall with sheaths of corn, and remember her when the sky shines with the perfect blue of a summer's day. She is with us as we explore how we co-create with Mother Earth.

Soil Components

Since soil is so complex and so important, an understanding of what lives there is crucial in creating a vibrant garden. It is also important to know what kind of soil you have in addition to having a felt sense of your soil's energy.

There are three kinds of particles that make up dirt: sand, silt, and clay. The balance of these particles determines how well the soil retains water and supports nutrients and microbes. Most soils are a combination of these particles. A combination of sand, silt, and clay is called loam.

To identify the type of soil you have, rub some moist soil between your fingers. Sand feels gritty, while silt feels smooth, and clay feels sticky. Now squeeze a moistened ball of dirt in your hand. Sand or sandy loam will break with slight pressure. Silty loam stays together but changes shape easily, and clay loam resists breaking when squeezed.

The soil type can also be determined by observing how well it absorbs water. Dig a cubic-foot-sized hole and let it dry completely over a few days (cover with a tarp if rain is due or your climate is dewy in the mornings), then fill the dry hole with water and monitor how long it takes for the water to drain. Sandy soil will drain in less than five minutes, while clay soil can hold water for more than ten minutes, depending on how much silt the soil contains. Silt retains water, but not as much as clay.

Ideal garden soil varies, depending on what you wish to grow (and what your land wishes to grow), but gardeners generally aim for what is called humus. Humus is a balanced loam rich in organic matter. It drains well but retains moisture, contains lots of nutrients, and allows the right amount of air and water to penetrate the soil particles. To create humus, regardless of what kind of soil you have, you need to add organic matter, which is discussed more fully later.

Soil is like a plant's immune system, and like our own immune system it requires plentiful and balanced nutrients. To determine what nutrients and minerals are present in your soil and which ones need boosting, use a soil test kit. They are relatively inexpensive, available at good garden stores, and are a fun science experiment. Test your soil at the end of a season, long after applying any fertilizer, manure, or compost to the garden. Scoop three tablespoons of dirt from two to six inches below the surface, taking care to not touch the soil with your hands. Let it dry in a paper bag in indirect sunlight. Following the directions that came with your kit, mix the soil with the test solutions. Your test will tell you the soil's pH, or acid level, and the presence of nitrogen, phosphorus, and potash. Some tests include other crucial nutrients like calcium. I will discuss later how to amend and fertilize your soil as needed for optimum garden growth.

Many things affect the makeup of your soil, from weather and climate to the history of the land. These variables determine what aggregates form in a given place, and also who lives there. Earthworms, bacteria, and other earthy creatures have a big affect on soil. Healthy populations of these earth allies mean a healthy garden.

Earth Ally: Worms

There are 1,800 known species of earthworms. Most garden worms are one of four kinds: night crawlers, red worms, manure worms, and garden or field worms. Worms plow the soil underground by eating decaying vegetation and dirt. They bore tunnels in the soil, allowing the air needed by microorganisms and roots to penetrate the soil. What worms don't use for their own energy is excreted as worm castings, which are full of nitrogen, phosphorus, calcium, and magnesium, all necessary nutrients for living soil.

Worms till thousands of pounds of soil per acre each year. By tilling so much soil and turning organic matter into worm manure, these little annelids improve soil fertility. They fertilize and enliven the soil just by going about their business, providing an invaluable service to gardeners. Their work affects bacteria populations, the porousness of the soil, and overall soil health. Cindy Hale of the University of Minnesota points out, "Worms are literally ecosystem engineers. They are at the base of the ecosystem. Their actions drive everything else that happens."[2]

Worms are hermaphroditic, sacred to Hermes. The messenger of the gods, Hermes rules over communication, profit, travel, and the crossroads. He leads the dead into the Underworld. Originally he was joined with Aphrodite, giving us the term *herm-aphrodite,* god and goddess in one. Worms bring a gender balance to the foundation of every garden.

"Worms are redeemers," writes Amy Stewart in *The Earth Moved*. "They move through waste and decay in their contemplative way, sifting, turning it into something else, something that is better."[3]

In what ways might worm energy help you in sifting through your own life and bringing about transformation? How might they bring nutrition and balance into your garden—the one in the soil and the larger garden of life?

Earth Ally: Microorganisms

Living soil contains billions of microorganisms that affect soil and plant health. These include bacteria, fungi, protazoa, and nematodes.

A teaspoon of fertile soil can contain up to one billion bacteria. Bacteria help the soil decompose organic matter, retain nutrients in the soil, compete with disease-causing organisms, and break down soil pollutants. Some bacteria help transfer nitrogen into the soil from legumes, improving soil quality. In our age of sterility and control, bacteria have gotten a bad name, but in truth all healthy ecosystems, including our own bodies, contain much beneficial bacteria. Provide beneficial bacteria with plenty of organic matter and you will have happy worms, dirt, and plants—

which means a healthy and bountiful garden.

Fungi, microorganisms that are slightly larger than bacteria, serve a similar function. They help decompose carbon compounds, making carbon available to plants and soil microbes, and help retain nutrients in the soil. They bind soil particles into aggregates, making the soil more porous to air and water. They provide food for other microorganisms, compete with plant pathogens, and decompose some types of pollution. Open a rotting log and you can see fungi at work, their long white strands eating away at the decomposing matter. Fungi in the soil, however, are often too small to see with the naked eye.

One form of fungus is called mycorrhizae, meaning fungus-root. These fungi form a symbiotic relationship with plant roots, improving the roots' absorption of water, air, and nutrients. In turn, the fungi receive sugars from the roots. Good soil containing lots of organic matter, water, air, and microorganisms leads to healthy mycorrhizal growth.

Protozoa, another microbial soil ally, primarily eat bacteria, releasing the fertilizing waste product ammonium in the soil and simultaneously stimulating bacteria populations. They also provide a food source for nematodes, an unsegmented worm. Nematodes are primarily beneficial, though some feed on roots and can kill a plant. Beneficial nematodes feed on protozoa, bacteria and fungi as well as other nematodes, including the harmful varieties. Like protozoa, they also release ammonium into the soil as a byproduct of their feeding. They distribute bacteria and fungi through the soil as they travel through their earthy domain.

Microorganisms and worms are not the only creatures who contribute to the makeup and health of garden soil. When creating a garden, you also play an important role in creating the composition of the soil by adding compost and other amendments.

Conscious Co-Creation

"In a world in which the life of the soil is everywhere under assault, building soil fertility can be a profound act of worship."

Starhawk[4]

Most garden soil in the Northern Hemisphere needs a bit of tweaking to achieve ideal pH, healthy levels of microorganisms, and amounts of organic matter to grow our favorite flowers and veggies. Even growing all native plants (which most people do not do, especially if you are growing food) may call for some soil amending, like loosening the soil and mixing in organic matter. Gardening often begins with working amendments into the soil like manure, compost, and peat moss. Think of amendments as gifts to your soil, rather than as a fix for bad dirt, which is often how fertilizers are presented. Rob Proctor, Artistic Director of Denver Botanical Gardens, said, "I've known people who have spent thirty years amending their clay soil and never enjoyed their garden; then they died. What was the point?"[5] Let your soil amendment be part of your co-creation with the land, a fun process of magic-making where you allow the soil to express its nature.

Sacred gardening is about acting consciously, with reverence for the soil and garden allies. When adding amendments like compost and peat moss, do so with the awareness that you nourish a process. When working with your soil to achieve the ideal mix for plants, you mix a magic potion of life. You participate in the grand dance of nourishing, mothering, and goddessing.

In addition to the traditional soil amendments and fertilizers, you might nourish your soil in other ways as well: pour some of your moon blood on the earth, sing to the land, put your nail clippings and hair into the compost pile. When my baby was born, I poured breast milk on the soil in thanks for the amazing gift the Mother had given me.

How can you be an active participant in the creation of your garden, not just in chemistry but in heart? Remember always that your soil and the beings that live there resonate with each other and with every cell in your body. Continue to look for ways to make this connection conscious and to respond to what you learn from the unseen beings of the soil.

GODDESS

Pachamama

The great Dragon Mother, Pachamama taught the Incan peoples to cultivate corn. When her people were secure in their knowledge of agriculture, she returned to her home in the Andes Mountains, where she may cause an earthquake or two by rubbing against the great stone walls of her palace. She presides over agriculture, and women sing and pray to her as we work in our gardens or tend the fields.[6]

Today, Pachamama has become a symbol for the wisdom of the indigenous peoples of South America; when we sprinkle cornmeal on the earth in honor of this mother goddess, we honor these people as well.[7]

Compost

My all-time favorite soil amendment is compost. Compost epitomizes the creativity and fertility of the earth, where grass clippings, wood ash, apple cores, and eggshells magically transform into fertile, rich soil. Like soil, compost is a knot of many interconnected relationships, illustrating the infinite creativity of the earth. The word *compost* comes from the Latin *componere*, "to put together." This "black gold" of waste, water, air, and microorganisms performs a juicy process that yields fertile soil.

While you can purchase compost from garden centers, making your own saves money and connects you directly with your garden. Creating your own compost not only ensures that you know exactly what goes into your soil—commercial compost is not regulated in many states and can include just about anything, including high-salt manure and weed seeds—it also establishes an immediate relationship between you and your garden as your trees, vegetables, flowers, and lawn benefit directly from your actions. Some of your household waste and the waste from your yard directly nourishes your garden, the food that grows there, and your body, soul, and community. Composting reduces our negative impact on the land by keeping kitchen and yard waste out of landfills. By composting, you participate in nature's laws of cycling and recycling.

Beginning the soil-building process with compost is a crucial first step in building a healthy garden, as compost boosts soil nutrient levels, encourages beneficial bacteria, and improves soil condition. Additional fertilizers cannot be absorbed by plants without help from soil microorganisms, and soil microorganisms need lots of organic matter to thrive. By starting with rich compost, you create a habitat where microorganisms can help plants absorb whatever they need. Usually compost provides a balance of nitrogen, carbon, calcium, and other nutrients, but you may need to add additional fertilizer for certain crops known as heavy feeders, those plants that require large amounts of certain nutrients. (Compost is not, strictly speaking, a fertilizer. Fertilizers feed plants, while amendments, like compost, feed soil.)

To make your own compost, you need a bin at least three cubic feet large that allows for air flow. Old crates, ¾-inch wire mesh, and other strong but open material make the best walls for a compost bin. You can also build it out of a clean food-grade 50-gallon drum on a tumbler that you rotate daily; or take an old garbage can, drill holes in the sides for air flow, and bury the bottom a few feet in the ground. You can also simply create a pile in a corner of the garden. Choose a location that is handy to get to from the kitchen and the garden alike, and one that is easily accessible by water. If you have room, build several bins or piles and fill them one at a time.

In your bin or pile, layer grass clippings that have not been treated with chemicals, small amounts of leaf waste, wood ash, soil, herbivore feces, and kitchen scraps. Brown matter like dried grass, leaves, or sawdust provides carbon, while green matter like fresh leaves and kitchen waste provides nitrogen. Manure is, despite its color, a "green" compost material, and it is very high in nitrogen. You need a balance of carbon, nitrogen, water, and air to create the ideal condition for compost; most garden and kitchen waste is too high in carbon to decay rapidly, so adding a source of nitrogen like manure will help speed up the composting process. If you don't live near any farms or horse stables, manure and other nitrogen-rich amendments can be purchased at garden centers prebagged or in bulk.

Make sure your pile stays moist, about as wet as a wrung-out sponge. Turn it periodically to aerate and mix the ingredients. If you have a problem with neighborhood animals like dogs or raccoons, make sure you have a door and a solid latch on your bin to keep them out.

I do not add citrus or onions to my compost, for they tend to slow the decay process or simply decay more slowly than the rest of the pile, but if your pile generates enough heat and has just the right conditions, this will matter less. Do not add dog or cat feces, as they can contain disease bacteria. Do not add butter, other oils, or meat, all of which can rot anaerobically and attract pests, from salmonella to rats. Do not include diseased plants, noxious weeds, invasive vines, or seeds. If you have a lot of resinous matter like pine needles, use that as mulch around acid-loving plants like strawberries rather than include it in the compost, as it will slow or halt decay. Same with cedar shavings; use these as mulch only where you do not want other plants to grow, and never put them in your compost.

Another way to transform waste into gardening gold is a worm bin, in which our favorite little hermaphrodites break down food waste into worm castings. A worm bin acts like a living garbage disposal, transforming kitchen and paper waste into nutrient-rich soil. You can keep one indoors during the cooler months (they do not smell unless something goes wrong) or outside when above freezing. In milder climates, you can build one outside from cinder blocks to provide some insulation during cooler temperatures. If you have a space for it on an enclosed porch or a quiet corner of your kitchen, an indoor bin can be made out of a 5- or 10-gallon opaque plastic tub. Black or dark plastic or wood is ideal to reduce the amount of light that reaches the worms. To provide your worm colony with air, drill ⅛-inch holes about one inch apart all the way around the bin about a foot off the ground. Purchase red worms or brown-nose worms at a local feed, garden, or tackle store to introduce to your bin (regular garden worms will die in your bin because there is not enough soil). You will need about a pound of worms per pound of kitchen waste each week. Worms can double their population about every ninety days, so you shouldn't need to ever buy more. If your bin gets too crowded, help your neighbor set up a bin for her garden.

Fill the bottom of the bin with water-soaked paper—newspaper or untreated cardboard works well. Place your worms on this bedding, and then feed them cut-up kitchen scraps once a week (no bread, oils, or meat, just vegetables and fruit). Your bin may accumulate excess moisture from decaying plant matter; to absorb this moisture, pile more newspaper at the bottom of the bin. The worms will eat the newspaper as well; it may need to be replaced regularly. About twice a year, when the bedding material has been consumed, remove the castings from the bin. To do so, move the worms and all the bin's contents to one side of the bin. Pull out uneaten food waste and put these chunks on the empty side. In a few weeks the worms will finish any matter left in the castings and move over to the other side. Carefully remove the abandoned castings, sifting through them to make sure you don't remove any worms. Replenish the bin with wet bedding and thank the worms for their gift. You can use castings on your garden as you would compost. For more information on worm bins, see *Worms Eat My Garbage* by Mary Appelhof.

Another great way to add nutrients to the soil is to make compost tea. You can use either regular compost or create a separate pile of weeds and invasive vines that you did not put in your primary compost pile. When the pile has turned to compost, fill a burlap sack with the rich matter. Tie off the bag and place it in a clean garbage can; fill the can with water to cover the bag, and let it all sit for a couple of days to make "tea." Pour this tea onto flower and vegetable beds as a fertilizer. It offers a concentrated dose of the nutrients in compost but does not affect soil porousness as solid compost does.

Compost, worm manure, and compost tea are all natural ways to boost soil fertility. Add these to your soil regularly to grow a healthy garden. If you need to add purchased compost or manure to your beds (like when you first start working with a new garden), make sure it is organic and well rotted.

Additional Amendments

Compost may be all you need to achieve ideal garden humus, but sometimes additional amendments can meet specific plants' individual needs. There are many natural fertilizers available that feed the soil instead of feeding the plants as conventional fertilizers do. Healthy soil yields healthy, balanced plants. Natural fertilizers carry the power of their source's energy and provide complete support for soil and plants. Studies show that vegetables grown in organically amended soils contain dramatically more nutrients than those from chemically amended land. Conventional fertilizers also tend to contain petroleum products (many fertilizer companies are affiliated with the petroleum industry), so organic fertilizers help reduce our use of nonrenewable resources.

To determine which amendments are best for your soil, take a soil test, ask local nurseries or the extension office what they recommend for your area's soil, or quite simply ask the soil itself. Keep in mind that without a lot of organic matter in the soil via compost and composted manure, plants cannot absorb fertilizers effectively. The soil is not unlike your own body; if you eat well and drink lots of water, your digestive system can absorb supplements better. Build the soil first and protect it with mulch (any substance that covers the soil while allowing the flow of air and water), then add natural amendments.

Vegetable garden soil should be slightly acidic, but it will depend on the plant. Most vegetables prefer a slightly acidic soil, with a pH of 6.0 to 6.8; incidentally, the human body prefers a similar pH of close to 7. Flowers' acid preference can vary greatly (and changing the acidity of the soil can even produce different results in the same plant, like determining the color of the flower); a plant guide can help steer you in the right direction for whatever flowers you wish to grow. You can make your soil more acidic (lower the pH) by adding composted manure, about 2 cubic feet of manure for each 100 square feet of garden. To raise the pH (or make the soil more alkaline), mix in 5 to 10 pounds of dolomitic lime for each 100 square feet; sandy soil requires less lime while loam and clay need more. Lime can be found at garden centers.

On a package of fertilizer, you will find a number indicating the ratio of nitrogen (N) to phosphorus (P) to potash or potassium (K). Traditionally only these three are listed, but many of the organic amendments that balance N, P, and K levels also add trace minerals like calcium and iron. Here are suggestions for giving back missing minerals to the soil, and the plants that need these nutrients in high amounts:

- cotton meal, coffee grounds, or alfalfa or green clover planted as a cover crop and worked into the soil, for nitrogen—corn, potatoes, brassicae (cabbage family), cucumbers, leafy greens, and onions need high amounts of nitrogen. Add these amendments regularly, as nitrogen is a key nutrient in the garden.
- egg shells, dolomitic lime, or wood ash for calcium—legumes need an extra boost.
- kelp meal for potassium, iron, and trace minerals; wood ash, granite dust, and greensand for potassium—brassicae, corn, potatoes, tomatoes, eggplant, and peppers need lots of potassium, and brassicae, leafy greens, and the tomato family need plenty of iron. Bone and blood meal also contain iron but are from animals killed in slaughterhouses, so I personally stay away from them. Kelp meal is also a natural fungicide.
- limestone (especially dolomitic lime) to raise the soil pH and add calcium and magnesium—needed by grains, corn, and the tomato family.

Add amendments at the beginning of a season, then let the garden breathe for a few days before planting. To reduce future nutrient imbalance, rotate crops each season. Crop rotation means that one year you might plant corn in a plot, then the next year plant legumes to replace nitrogen, and the following year plant tomatoes. This assures the soil has a chance to recover from the previous year's crop. Mix compost and worm castings into the soil periodically throughout the season and before planting a new crop. Add mulch to the soil surface to reduce nutrient runoff.

Earth Ally: Arthropods

Soil fertility is also affected by arthropods, powerful allies that often get a bad reputation as creepy crawlies. Arthropods include millipedes, spiders, ants, and other insects with jointed legs and an exoskeleton. They help by decomposing plant matter, preying on other insects, and eating fungi, worms, and other arthropods. Their burrows aerate the soil while their fecal pellets provide fertilizer. They eat disease-causing organisms and contribute to a healthy food web. Sacred to Arachne and Ariadne, spider goddesses that guide mortals along the webs of fate, spiders and ants can teach us much about our own hearts as they weave together the dreams of the world.

According to the *Medicine Cards* by Jamie Sams and

David Carson, Ant teaches us about patience—an important lesson for a gardener. Ants live in a matriarchal society and dedicate their lives to serving the Queen. They work hard, building the community and their home bit by bit. They teach us trust in the universe: all will be provided. If you find yourself in a period where patience and faith are thin, spend some time observing ants in your garden.

Ants are industrious creatures, and in their pursuit for food they may find their way into our houses. Instead of spraying them with Raid, take a moment to communicate with them. Nonhuman creatures may not speak our verbal language, but they can be communicated with through energy, words, and intention. Go to where the ants are entering your home, or find some outside, and speak to them as you would another human. While you speak, visualize in your mind what you would like to happen. Ask them to please stay outside your home—they wouldn't want you in theirs. Offer to leave some food and water outside in times of drought. Be firm and persistent, and in time your problem should abate. I will discuss communication with nonhumans in greater detail later on.

You can also gently encourage ants to avoid areas like your kitchen counters by spraying the area—not the ants—with an infusion of peppermint or tea tree oil. This spray disinfects, smells great, and repels unwanted arthropod guests. Mix ten to fifteen drops of oil per quart spray bottle of water, and spray the area where unwanted ants are found. When ants swarm in the garden, leave them alone. When I worked at a greenhouse one summer, it saddened and amazed me how many people purchased poisons to kill ants in their yard. There is absolutely no reason to do so; respect the ants' home and they will respect yours.

Ant's cousin Spider teaches us about integration, weaving together all we know and sense. "Spider is the symbol for the infinite possibilities of creation," write Sams and Carson.[8] What could happen were we to weave together the powers of love and creativity so powerful yet so isolated here on earth? By listening to Spider, we learn about the feminine force of creation, of weaving together the world. Sams and Carson continue, "The most important message from Spider is that you are an infinite being who will continue to weave the patterns of life and living throughout time. Do not fail to see the expansiveness of the eternal plan."[9] In gardening, you participate in the great creation of a powerful, Goddess-blessed world; in honoring Spider in your garden, you can learn how to weave as a co-creator of life.

Sacred Sister: Rebecca Dye

landscape architect

I first heard of Rebecca Dye through Elizabeth Murray's *Cultivating Sacred Spaces,* where Dye talks about her work with stones in landscapes. Dye runs a landscape architecture and environmental design firm with her husband, Hank Helbush, in Saratoga, California. Their focus is on habitat restoration and historical renovation; in both large-scale landscapes and private gardens, they seek to remove invasive plants, welcome the spirit of the place, and create a garden or landscape that resonates with its own essence.

Rebecca enjoys working with large stones, which not only provide beauty to a landscape but also offer a grounding and rooting influence. She relates to the stones as beings. In *Cultivating Sacred Space,* she says,

> The rocks provide that power—to stabilize the energy that had dissipated off the site—even when they first arrive before they are set. The whole energy of the property changes. Everyone notices it. We all get incredibly thirsty ... It's a natural biological connection, and we all feel how the energy changes instantly. When the rocks are unloaded, everyone talks softly. It's like a Presence has arrived.[10]

When I contacted Rebecca about her work, she told me a story about the power of honoring the garden. A family hired Hank and Rebecca to landscape their property, but Rebecca was hesitant to work with them at first as they seemed more interested in having a perfect lawn in a perfect suburban environment than working with the land. As she spent some time with the woman of the family, she discovered that secretly this mother wanted a special play place for her children. So Rebecca and Hank designed a play yard, including the family in the design process. With the children they released praying mantis and ladybugs, both beneficial predators, helping the children understand rather than fear these garden allies. Rebecca said, "The children learned that fruit comes from trees and that abstract play with sand and dirt and water can be really cool."

The mother of the family began to discover herself by no longer using chemicals on her lawn, growing strawberries in the yard, and talking directly to any unhealthy trees on her land. The trees and the woman blossomed from this new relationship.

Shortly after Hank convinced the couple to save a large bay tree on their property, he saw a nature spirit for the first time, a "flaming light turning and twisting like smoke" moving through the trees of the family garden. The family and the land were growing together.

After a time, the family decided to buy some land that had been an apple orchard but had stood neglected for a decade. The father wanted to build a multimillion-dollar home with a swimming pool, which would have required the removal of 90 percent of the old apple trees. It would reduce the habitat for hawks and owls, redwood trees, and willow seedlings. The architects spent time on the land with the family, teaching them about the marsh land and the apple trees, and the father decided to give up his plans in favor of the wildness of the land and the orchard. They decided instead to fix up the old farmhouse.

Several years later, Rebecca ran into the mother, who told her that her husband had become an organic apple farmer and that the sacred was an everyday part of their lives. She held nature classes for school kids at the orchard, and said her own children were flourishing. About this woman's metamorphosis and the change in her family, Rebecca wrote, "She created the vessel, the chalice, the field of safety that opened the door for the sacred to be allowed in and experienced not only by her husband and children but now by many children, parents, families, and friends. Because of this, she's touched the lives and altered the values of many people."[11]

Working with the land and respecting it as sacred can completely transform the way one lives her life. When you work in the garden, remember to work *with* the land and to honor the natural forces and processes present.

GODDESS

Pani

TRICKSTER RONGO-MAUI stole the sweet potato from his sky brother Whanui. Hiding it in his loin cloth, he returned to earth and impregnated his wife Pani. She gave birth to sweet potato in a stream; to this day she cultivates the sweet potato patch in the Underworld.[12]

This Maori goddess rules over plants and fertility; honor her when you plant root crops by sprinkling a little saltwater on the soil in honor of her Maori heritage.

Working the Soil

In addition to adding compost and other amendments, a gardener needs to fluff up and aerate the soil to make it more porous for water and air. The conventional way to do this is to till the top few layers of soil, but this practice actually strips the rich topsoil and damages microbial populations. Instead, double digging or simple aeration of the soil by poking it with a pitchfork maintains the soil's fertility. Adding mulch on top of the carefully worked soil helps keep moisture in and extreme heat away from plants' roots.

The first year I begin a plot, I usually choose to double-dig the soil if it has been packed down and ignored for years. This method retains natural, living soil levels while aerating and loosening soil much deeper than conventional tilling. It also raises the soil level, giving you a raised bed with greater surface area than a flat plot. Raised beds help keep the soil warm—useful in areas prone to mold. They also improve drainage and soil consistency. You end up with happier plants, more planting space, and fewer weeds. In arid climates, you may want to build a wall around your raised bed to conserve water by reducing evaporation and to keep the soil cool. Depending on how you want your garden to look and the space you have to work with, beds can be any shape, including a traditional rectangle, a spiral, or a keyhole shape, round with a path down the middle for access.

To double dig, you will need a spade; a wheelbarrow or tarp; compost; manure or peat moss; and a pitchfork. Announce to the land a day in advance that you will be disturbing the soil so that microorganisms and worms can prepare. The living creatures of the soil can hear you and will respond to the energy and intention of what you say. Ask the land if double digging is the best course of action; you may be told that you need only aerate this area by poking the tines of a pitchfork into the soil, which allows in air and water without disturbing soil layers. If the soil agrees that double digging is the best action, then proceed the following day or whenever the land instructs you to do so.

First, determine where you wish to place your garden space, based on available light and water. A ten-foot-wide bed can be harvested easily from either side, so don't make your bed any wider than that. At one end of your bed, dig a trench one spade deep, one foot wide and as long as your bed. Put the dirt from this trench into your wheelbarrow or onto the tarp. With the pitchfork, poke down another foot—or as deeply as possible—into the soil to aerate. Do not turn or otherwise disturb this soil. Dig another trench next to the first and lift that soil into the first trench. You can add compost now into each newly filled trench, or you can add it all as a surface treatment sifted into the newly aerated soil at the end. Keep digging and turning trenches and poking into the undersoil until you reach the end of your bed, and fill the last trench with the soil from the first. If you have not added compost as you go, now spread compost, manure, peat moss, and other amendments onto the surface of the soil. Using your pitchfork, sift the amendments into the softened soil. Shape your bed and very loosely pat everything down. Move slowly and deliberately, listening to the essence of the soil as you work. When you finish, invite the worms and other allies back in to the soil. Let it sit for a few days or weeks before planting—this is a great activity to do early in the spring when you cannot put in seeds but are anxious to get into the garden, or in the fall if you have begun a new bed space.

The following year, simply aerate your bed with a solid, sharp pitchfork. Poke it into the soil of your garden beds as deep as it will go and gently lean back to loosen the soil without disturbing plant roots or soil layers. Pull the fork out and push it into the soil again a few inches away. Repeat throughout your bed, wherever you wish to plant. Aerate at the end of the growing season, and again in the spring before you plant. This will help prevent compacting without disturbing the natural balance in the living soil. Worms prefer undisturbed soil (because bacteria prefer undisturbed soil with lots of air and organic matter), so aerating without tilling or digging will make your garden a more attractive home to these powerful allies.

Another method for improving soil fertility and consistency each year is to layer seed-free mulch on the soil and around your plants. Mulch includes any organic matter covering the soil such as hay, leaves, or grass clippings, and it helps soil to retain moisture and maintain a steady temperature. Heavy mulching with many layers mimics nature's way of forming soil and provides soil allies with lots of nutrients. Put mulch around seedlings, add mulch throughout the growing season as needed, and heavily mulch a bed in the fall.

You may decide that double digging is too much work, and instead create a bed by aerating the soil as described above, then constructing a bed entirely out of piled mulch, layering compost and different kinds of mulch until the bed is at least a foot thick. Between each layer of mulch, include a layer of compost. You can plant right in this mix, adding mulch around the base of plants as the layers settle and decompose; this technique is often referred to as "lasagna gardening" because of the layering process.

The time it takes to double dig, aerate, or mulch your garden bed provides a marvelous opportunity for a moving meditation. As you dig, lift, turn, and amend the soil, you get to know its essence more deeply. Open your senses as you work, and sink into present awareness. Stay present to your breath, the smells and sounds around you, the consistency of the dirt, and anything else you notice. You may find that your body remembers an ancient dance with the land cultivated by our ancestors thousands of years ago. You may begin to hear the song of the land more clearly. A garden prepared with consciousness of our relationship with the earth produces plants with greater life-force energy.

Are you beginning to hear the story of soil and its relationship with you as the gardener? What else does it have to teach you? What does soil tell you about yourself? Remember that you are of the earth. As you dig, keep this in your awareness. Record your thoughts in your journal by writing or sketching.

GODDESS

Cailleach Beara

The goddess of the changing seasons, Cailleach Beara is the divine ancestor of Scotland. She blesses corn crops and watches over natural springs. Whenever she is tired of being an old woman, she renews her own youth, just as the earth does each year.

Cailleach Beara's strength is legendary, and it is said she formed Stonehenge and Newgrange by dropping stones from her apron. Many of the lakes, rivers, and mountains throughout the British Isles were formed by her divine touch.[13]

In Scotland, *cailleach* refers to the last sheaf harvested in the fall; for blessings through the winter, tie a ribbon around a sheaf of corn or tall grass, and hang it on a nail near the door.

Earth Ally: Gnomes

The north and the earth element are associated with gnomes, the guardians of the earth. In Greek, *gnoma* means "knowledge" or "the knowing ones." While the maiden Snow White's companions are known as dwarves, they epitomize gnome energy as miners of jewels, protectors of the forest, and keepers of secrets.

The best thing you can do to keep your land's gnomes happy is to treat the earth with respect. Offer them gifts of gemstones, like amethyst, tourmaline, and crystal. Ask them what your land needs, and listen carefully to the answers. Gnomes are the consciousness of minerals themselves; as you add nutrients to your soil, call on them to awaken the powers of strength and fertility in the garden. These elementals are very practical and can aid you in material matters like money, soil, and your home.[14]

Gnomes can help you communicate with the animal allies of the living garden. Ask for their guidance as you expand your awareness to include worms, bugs, and microorganisms. Let your awareness settle and ground; to communicate with earth beings, you must resonate with earth rhythms.

Where to Plant, and When

Increase your success in the garden and enhance your own attunement to the natural flow of the seasons by gardening in synchrony with the powers that be: the sun, Earth, and moon. These bodies determine when and where and how to plant your garden. Plants follow the rhythm of the earth and sun, their life cycle attuned precisely to the length of the day and the temperature of the soil and air. Like tides, plants also naturally respond to the pull of the moon, as they contain so much water.

Again, keen observation leads to greater gardening success. Throughout the year, spend time outside each day and every evening to notice when and where the sun rises and sets, the shifting cast of shadows, and freezing patterns. In spring, watch the trees and bushes, observing their timing of sprouting and bloom. Take the temperature of your soil frequently in the spring or whenever you plan to plant; each plant has a preferred soil temperature for ideal germination. Learn your last and first average dates of frost, found in the newspaper, online, or by contacting your local plant nursery or extension office. With this information, you will know when to start seeds indoors, when to move transplants into the garden or start seeds outdoors, and where your plants can use extra help like a coldframe (a box with a glass or fiberglass lid that provides protection from frost, snow, and wind during the cooler months).

Notice which parts of your garden might be a separate microclimate, a spot that is different from the prevailing climate. Microclimates might include reflected heat from a stone wall, the shade of a tree, or a cool and wet gully. Soil temperatures and water levels will differ in these areas. Look for warmer spots and reflected light for plants like tomatoes and peppers, and seek dappled light or moister soil for plants that crave cool, like spinach and peas. You can even create your own microclimates by incorporating small ponds to reflect light, building mounds to create areas of shade and sun, or removing and planting shrubs and trees. For a detailed discussion of microclimates, refer to Toby Hemenway's *Gaia's Garden*.

Observing shade, sun, water, and microclimates throughout the year will help you garden year-round by allowing you to match plants' needs to the available resources. A greenhouse or a coldframe can further extend your planting and harvesting period beyond frost. A simple winter greenhouse can be constructed out of a sturdy frame and plastic sheeting. Place your greenhouse or coldframe in a spot that gets plenty of winter sunlight, and be sure to monitor for overheating or drying out. Plant seeds in your frame in the fall for winter greens and at the end of winter for an early spring harvest (I'll discuss seed germination more fully in chapter 3: Fire). Due to the lack of summer pests and weeds, a coldframe takes very little tending and provides for a splendid winter salad. Just a few of the vegetables well suited to a coldframe include root veggies, salad greens, asparagus, parsley, and onions. You can also use your coldframe to get a jump on the warm season by using it as a nursery for plants like tomatoes.

An even easier way to grow cool season crops is with a row cover, a clear plastic or cloth cover draped over short supports along a row or part of a row. Inverted U-shaped medium-gauge wire, tall enough to clear the tops of crops, makes a simple and inexpensive support. Secure ends of the plastic cover with rocks or by burying an inch or two. During the heat of the day, vent by pulling the edge of your cover back. Row covers and coldframes can also be purchased at many garden stores, online at seeds ofchange.com or Common Ground Garden Supply (see Resources).

For more information on winter gardening and a full list of cool-season vegetables, see Eliot Coleman's *Four-Season Harvest*.

An even deeper relationship with the land can be explored through your inner knowing. A sacred sister takes time to listen directly to her plants, sensing their individual light, warmth, and gravitational needs. All gardens have their own personality as well as their own microclimates, so listening to the garden itself is key in determining when to plant, harvest, and perform other tasks. Get to know your own land's rhythms and quirks by listening with your whole self.

To feel the rhythm of your land, place your hands on the largest tree in the yard, one on either side of the trunk. Feel into the tree and notice what you feel in your hands. You may also see energy or hear it as a rhythm or tone. You may feel two pulses, the spiral going around the tree sunwise and the spiral going between the earth and the tree. When you get a sense of these rhythms and any other information, move to another plant. Ask the plants and the garden when to plant, prune, and fertilize. After you have checked in with a scattering of plants, you will have a good idea of when and where it will be best to plant and the special needs of each plant or area.

The Moon

"And when the Moon says
'It is time to
Plant,'
Why not dance,
Dance and
Sing?"

Hafiz[15]

It is not only the sun that determines the best time to plant a garden, but also our closest celestial neighbor, the moon. For thousands of years, wise women have gardened in tune with the moon. Consider the difference in light under a full moon versus when the moon is dark, and how the moon creates Earth's tides, and you will have an idea of the value of gardening with Luna. Plants and the human body consist largely of water; though the pull is subtle, we are as affected by the moon's gravity as the oceans.

Gardening with the moon depends on two rhythms: light and gravity, determined by her journey around Earth. To plant with the phases of the moon, note if your seeds are short, long, or extra-long germinating. Plant information on the back of seed packs includes how long it will take the seeds to germinate. Short-germinating seeds, like beans and lettuce, will germinate in one to seven days. Long germination means eight to twenty-one days, and includes celery and garlic. Some plants take up to twenty-eight days to germinate, known as extra-long germinating seeds.

You want to put seeds in the earth, or germinate them indoors (more on this in chapter 3: Fire) so that they will germinate near the new moon, when the moon's earthward pull is strongest. This pull helps the new plant establish strong root growth. According to the biodynamic method of farming, short- and extra-long germinating seeds should be planted from two days before to seven days after the new moon. Long-germinating seeds and seedlings should be planted or transplanted at the full moon and up to seven days after full. These planting times take advantage of the gravitational and magnetic pull of the moon as well as levels of moonlight and give the seeds the optimum situation for their germination.[16]

Other gardening activities can be attuned to the moon as well. At the new moon, prune to encourage growth. During the full moon, harvest herbs used for magic or healing, and pick fruits and vegetables for enhanced flavor. The waning moon is a time of settling and letting go; use this crone time as the moon's energy settles back into the earth to harvest root vegetables, weed, and prune to inhibit growth. During the dark of the moon, when lunar energy is deep in the earth, take time to renew and be still. This is the time of going into the cave to meditate.

The Labyrinth

"The labyrinth is truly a tool for transformation. It is a crucible for change, a blueprint for the sacred meeting of psyche and soul, a field of light, a cosmic dance. It is a center for empowering ritual."

Lauren Artress[17]

Gardening is not just about growing food; it's also about taking time to reconnect with spirit. A powerful tool for meditation and reconnection is the labyrinth, an ancient symbol of going within and being reborn. While you do not need anything special to meditate and connect with spirit or with earth allies, having a spot dedicated to spiritual practice can help motivate and support your journey of awareness. A labyrinth leads one to communion with spirit through meditative movement. Walking the labyrinth's spirals connects your feet with the earth, centering and grounding your body and spirit. It aligns you with your path as a spiritual gardener.

A labyrinth in the garden adds beauty and a spiritual focal point. You can shape it out of stones, mulched pathways, little lights, or even rope. If you have a patio, consider painting a labyrinth right on the concrete or forming one out of tiles. Even a platter-sized labyrinth carved in wood or plaster can be traced by your finger as you sit in your garden. You might follow the classic or medieval labyrinth shapes, or form a simple spiral, which lends almost the same meditative qualities as the twists of a labyrinth.

When you include a labyrinth in your garden or home, you call upon ancient powers of contemplation and magic. People have walked labyrinths for over four thousand years. Originally a pagan metaphor for the life path, the labyrinth now snakes her way through mystical or contemplative Christian worship as well. It can be a lovely representation of non-sectarian worship, honoring all our ancestors. It mimics the womb, the brain, and other vortex shapes in nature.

Greek mythology tells the story of how Theseus killed the dreaded Minotaur, who was trapped in a great labyrinth, with help from the princess Ariadne. In pre-Grecian versions of the myth, King Minos was actually the God of Death, and his labyrinth of death and rebirth was presided over by the goddess Ariadne. The labyrinth was her dancing ground. The Greeks retold the story to fit their more patriarchal culture, one that feared death. By slaying the Minotaur, Theseus destroyed death.[18]

Gardeners know the value of death and have faith in the rebirth of the world each spring. A labyrinth in the garden can be a visual reminder of the Wheel of the Year and the turning of the seasons. Walking the spirals helps a gardener slow down internally so she is better able to attune with the gentle unfolding of nature.

Making a labyrinth calls on the powers of the left brain, while walking it relies on the creative and mystical gifts of the right brain. The labyrinth takes us on a meandering but determined path, and the thinking brain has to let go as you spiral in and out in a seemingly random journey. There is one way in and one way out—much like life. The labyrinth reminds us to take one step at a time, putting one foot in front of the other. You might sit for a while before and after walking the path to still yourself and open to present awareness.

At the center of the labyrinth's vortex you meet your inner self and the Goddess within. Like the heart of a conch or the deepest blood beat of the womb, you return to your most primal, beautiful self. In the center is a still place that allows one to release the past and let go of the future, to call on the God of Death for help with letting go. Let go into the labyrinth, into the curls of the earth, and listen. It is here you will find your sacred self.

GODDESS

Persephone

QUEEN OF THE Underworld, Persephone is the crone form of the triple goddess. Her counterparts are Demeter the mother and Kore the maiden.[19]

She leads us into the cave, the dark moon time, the labyrinth of death and discovery. In a culture where activity and light rule, we can call on Persephone to remind us of our inner knowing and the wisdom of the dark.

Gardeners know her gifts well, for we understand that for life to thrive there must be death. Ask her to bless your compost pile, your soil, and the blessings of death that beget life.

Earth Magic: Local Organic Gardening

"For gardeners to be on the forefront of a better relationship between humans and nature seems only natural."

Toby Hemenway[20]

Sacred gardening is not only about having a personal spiritual relationship with the land, it's also about bringing our work out into the world. It is our role as women of the garden to reweave the strands of life that have been broken or lost for so long. In each chapter of this book, I will offer suggestions for what actions you might take in rebuilding a society based on respect for the land, community, and interdependence—the laws of the natural world that our dominant culture more or less ignores. You may also find other ways of serving the sacred land that I do not include here; we each have our own gifts to offer. Certain actions, however, are foundational to transformational gardening. One of them is to garden and farm sustainably, without the use of pollutants and dangerous chemicals. Not only does the planet demand it, but energy resources and the health of all life insist that we convert our food production and all other cultivation to organic.

Organically grown food is much more nutritious than conventionally grown vegetables. A study in the UK found that organic produce contains much higher amounts of magnesium, vitamin C, phosphorus, and iron than those conventionally grown.[21] Conventionally grown beans have one-tenth the iron of organic beans, while conventional spinach contains half the calcium of organic spinach.[22] Organic lettuce, cabbage, spinach, and potatoes contain particularly high levels of minerals. We absorb nutrients through food far better than through vitamin supplements, and vitamin deficiencies can lead not only to physical health problems but depression and anxiety as well.

Danish researchers found significantly higher amounts of antioxidants—from 10 to 50 percent more—in organically grown produce.[23] Antioxidants reduce our risk of developing cancers and coronary heart disease. A study in Sweden suggests that consuming organic foods may reduce the prevalence of allergies as well.[24]

Not only does organic food contain more nutrients but also a lot less poison than conventionally grown produce. The Pesticide Action Network North America (PANNA) found, when they examined data collected by the Centers for Disease Control and Prevention (CDC), that essentially all Americans contain in our bodies a cocktail of dangerous pesticides.[25] While the EPA and CDC know some of the ill effects of individual chemicals, there are almost no studies demonstrating what might happen when these pesticides are combined. Our bodies have become living chemistry laboratories, containing toxic levels of dozens of kinds of dangerous chemicals.

The highest amounts of toxic pesticides were found in children, women, and Mexican Americans. The average six to eleven-year-old studied by the CDC is exposed to four times the "acceptable" level of the pesticide chlorpyrifos, a chemical known to interrupt nerve development in humans.[26] Women had extremely high levels of organchlorine pesticides in their blood and urine samples, chemicals that inhibit brain and neural development in fetuses when they cross the placenta.[27] Not just women are affected: Men who consume primarily chemically treated produce have a lower sperm count than those who eat organic (and sperm are just one type of cell).[28]

Our bodies are not able to process or pass on many of the chemicals, pesticides, and other pollutants we are exposed to; over time, pesticides build to toxic levels. We store many of them in our fatty tissue, from which we draw extra nutrients for breast feeding. Breast milk contains extremely high levels of pollutants.[29] Furthermore, a study in the UK found that women diagnosed with breast cancer are five to nine times more likely to have pesticide residue in their blood.[30] By buying and growing organic foods, you are protecting your children and voting for the protection and health of women, men, and children everywhere.

Of course, it is not only humans who are adversely affected by pesticides. Reducing the production of conventionally grown produce reduces our negative impact on wildlife and plant populations. According to the Worldwatch Institute, converting one percent of United States' lawns to organic garden space "would reduce the toxic pesticide exposure to families and wildlife by up to 3.4 million kilograms per year, while also helping to reduce reliance on energy-intensive commercial food transport."[31] What if every fourth house converted its lawn to a pesticide-free garden? That might be 20 percent of existing lawn in the United States, translating to 68 million kilograms less toxic pesticide exposure in food, soil, and water. That means healthier children, water, and wildlife. It means living more respectfully toward the natural world—including us humans.

One study found a strong association between home pesticide use, especially lawn treatment and pest extermination, and some types of childhood cancers.[32] The traditional American Dream may include acres of rolling jade-green lawns and a year-round produce selection at the local grocer, but does it include our children dying young of cancer?

In addition to growing organic fruits and vegetables on our own land, we can make a big difference by buying organic produce from local sources. Brian Halweil of the Worldwatch Institute writes, "A head of lettuce grown in the Salinas Valley of California and shipped nearly 3,000 miles to Washington, D.C., requires about 36 times as much fossil fuel energy in transport as it provides in food energy when it arrives."[33] Take that much inefficient use of fossil fuel out of the picture, and you end up with less reliance on ecologically harmful oil drilling and unstable Middle Eastern nations.

Furthermore, burning fossil fuel produces carbon dioxide, a molecule that traps heat on the earth and is largely responsible for the greenhouse effect. Organic gardening actually helps to reduce and even reverse these greenhouse gases accumulating in the atmosphere by collecting and retaining carbon in organic soil. The Rodale Institute determined, after a 23-year-long study, that organic soils help retain carbon, reducing and even reversing the overabundance of greenhouse gases in the atmosphere.[34] The UN estimated that in order to stabilize the climate at the current levels of warming (the planet has already heated a degree or more in the last decade from greenhouse gases), we would need to immediately reduce our fossil fuel use by sixty percent.[35] Growing locally and in tune with the local seasons and climate (by not growing hothouse tomatoes in December, for instance) could help go a long way toward this reduction of greenhouse gases, especially if done on a large scale.

Recently, Americans have been alerted to our vulnerability from bioterrorism and the spread of infections, like mad cow disease. By importing our food from around the world and shipping it across the country in large cargo containers, we put ourselves at risk for food tampering or delivery disruption by terrorists. We also bring in foreign pesticides, which may be controlled even less stringently than in the United States, as well as foreign diseases. The 2001 foot-and-mouth outbreak in the United Kingdom was traced to grain imported from China, and it spread rapidly via cows transported to central slaughterhouses.[36] Eating locally raised and locally, humanely slaughtered animals would have vastly reduced the risk of such an epidemic.

In the United States, most people get their produce from the supermarket. Most of the food in supermarkets comes from giant agribusiness conglomerates. These corporations control farms, acting as the only purchaser of the farmer's produce as well as the supplier of the farmer's seed, fertilizer, and other supplies. That farmer sees very little of the money we pay at the supermarket; most of the purchase price of food goes to packaging and marketing.

That money, along with additional government subsidy, pays for chemical fertilizers and pesticides. Agriculture today is the largest polluter and uses the most petroleum of any industry. Its use of pesticides and cultivation of monoculture (an entire field of potatoes or broccoli) reduces biodiversity through habitat loss and accidental or intentional wildlife poisoning. Food diversity has also suffered worldwide, because agribusiness farms grow what is most hardy and least perishable—not what is healthiest or most flavorful.[37] Those foods can only be grown locally.

Local foods grown in your yard, in a community plot, or on a local organic farm keep money local. Buying locally ensures that small farms can avoid being folded into the oligopolistic agriculture market and losing control over their own land. Growing your own food keeps more funds in your pocket as you do not pay for shipping, packaging, or other extra costs—just the food and your time spent in the garden. Sharing your garden bounty with neighbors or shopping at the local farmers' market builds community; strong community means lower crime rates and individuals whose needs are met more efficiently.

Fred Kirshenmann, organic farmer, said, "Food is not like any other commodity. Food is a community creature. Food has always been at the center of community celebrations—a wedding, a birthday. So the industrial giants who want to completely commodify our food and reduce it to roughage for profit are bucking against a very powerful cultural phenomenon: hospitality. But true hospitality emerges when we each bring something to the table."[38]

When we each bring something grown by our own hands to the table, we teach our community and our children about true hospitality. Children who garden learn the value of cooperation and working with the land. They discover the joys and sorrows of the life cycle and responsibility for their actions. Children who garden eat more fresh vegetables, reducing their chances of becoming obese later in life; and gardening together teaches youth about cooperation, participation, and self-motivation. By sharing with their neighborhood, especially those in need, they learn about sharing and peace-making. They learn about compassion.

Organic, locally grown produce results in less cancer and heart disease, less obesity, reduced greenhouse gases, lower crime rates, and safer, healthier communities. You can truly make a big difference by growing and buying organic. Educate others on the power of chemical-free gardening by writing letters to the editor of your local paper and giving talks at local schools. What you cannot grow, purchase from local farmers or Community Supported Agriculture (CSA) programs. Eat seasonally to save money and live more in tune with the land; seasonal veggies taste better and have more nutritional value.

Organic gardening is a spiritual practice as well. As a steward of the sacred land, you not only believe the earth is sacred, you act in accordance with this belief. And as you evolve as a person, you will find that spirituality is not just in your head and heart, but in your hands and actions as well. Organic gardening is a simple but very powerful way to live in harmony with yourself, your community, and the planet.

Sacred Sister: Cheryl Rogowski

organic farmer

Cheryl Rogowski decided that growing hundreds of tons of a single type of crop and shipping it off to an unknown, faceless consumer no longer worked for her. In 1994, she introduced a crop of chili peppers to the family farm which had, until then, grown only wholesale onions. She also introduced organic practices to the farm.

Over the years, she expanded her business of organically grown vegetables to include many different types of crops. She found that running an unconventional farm, one that grew many types of organic vegetables, meant rewriting the way she did business. She realized that to be successful she would need to take on tasks not generally done by the farmers themselves, including marketing, educating consumers, and community action.

Cheryl arranged for weekly deliveries of her produce to local senior centers, mentored immigrant farmers from South America, started a catering business, sold her produce at farmers' markets, and became an activist for land reform. She now grows 250 varieties of produce on her farm while serving her community. For these efforts, she received a $500,000 Genius Award in 2004 from the John D. and Catherine T. MacArthur Foundation.[39]

Cheryl teaches us that we can change the ways things were done in the past. We can succeed as women walking our talk. She shows other farmers that organic farming may mean changing the face of agriculture—but with heart and conviction, it can be done.

Earth Resources

To find a local CSA:

Biodynamic Farming and Gardening Association. Inc.
Building 1002B,
Thoreau Center, The Presidio
P. O. Box 29135
San Francisco, CA 94129-0135
Phone (888) 516-7797
Fax (415) 561-7796

For a list of CSAs:
Phone (800) 516-7797

For supplies and resources, contact:

Common Ground Garden Supply and Education Center
559 College Avenue
Palo Alto, CA 94306
Phone (650) 493-6072

Common Ground also offers classes on permaculture, organic gardening, compost, and more.

Seeds of Change
seedsofchange.com
(888) 762-7333

Offers a free catalog of their unique organic seeds, books, and foods. A free online newsletter is also available, with articles about seed saving, organic agriculture, and permaculture.

For more information on organic gardening techniques, year-round gardening, and biodynamic farming, see:

Four-Season Harvest by Eliot Coleman (Chelsea Green Publishing, 1999)

How to Grow More Vegetables by John Jeavons (Ten Speed Press, 2002)

A great book on soil is *The Soul of the Soil* by Joe Smillie and Grace Gershuny. It is scientifically oriented and can help you spot any soil challenges.

NOTES

A very useful website on compost and soil is www.mastercomposter.com. Much of the information on worm bins I shared here with you I learned from this site.

For more on labyrinths, see "The Voice of the Labyrinth Movement" at www.veriditas.net, or contact:

Veriditas™
1009 General Kennedy Ave.
1st Floor, The Presidio
San Francisco, CA 94129
Phone (415) 561-2921
Fax (415) 561-2922
Email: contact@veriditas.net

Notes

CHAPTER 2

Air

it's the wind & the air

where our colors fly

so wave around your favorites

send your voices on high

it's not so much what

as always asking why

it's the wind & the air ...

Tony Edelblute,
"No Name Thing"

GODDESS

Isis

THIS SUPREME GODDESS of the Nile protected the Egyptian throne by surrounding the pharaoh with her great wings. A moon and sky goddess, she gifts us with transformation and rebirth.

To honor her in your garden and invoke her serenity and protection, fill a blue and gold bird bath with purified rain water. Place twenty-two stones around the base, representing the High Priestess tarot card. Anoint the base with sandalwood oil, and chant a blessing upon all of life as you sprinkle the water on your plants. Keep the water fresh for the birds, butterflies, and wasps to enjoy.

Who Is Breathing?

Listen now to the eastern winds as they bring to the garden their blessings. We follow the Celtic knot of the sacred garden into the twists and eddies of air. In the direction of the rising sun, the land of beginnings, you learn to think, to plan, and to communicate your ideas. Air, the element of the east, not only provides crucial nutrients to the physical garden, it offers inspiration in the garden of your mind and heart. Air teaches you about the gifts of the mind: imagination, music, intuition, and intellect. You must draw on all of these gifts to create a sacred garden.

Several languages have the same word for *air* and *spirit*; in Hebrew, *ruach* means wind, breath, mind, or spirit. Spiritual practices around the world use breath to deepen awareness, cleanse the mind and body, and enter into altered states. The breath is a bridge between conscious and unconscious, internal and external. As you inhale, you actively take the world into your body. You take in the gift of oxygen created by plants. On your exhale, you relax, release, and let go. Your exhale feeds the inhalation of your plants. In the exchange of breath, air teaches you about community and communication. David Hoffmann in *The New Holistic Herbal* writes,

> The air we breathe is spiritual ecology in action. When we draw in the breath of life, we share that air with all other human beings, all life on our planet. It is through respiration that our oneness with the trees becomes a manifest fact, and our communion with the oceans has immediate impact.... From the perspective of spiritual ecology

we can repeat the question of the mystics: 'Who is breathing?'[40]

Before embarking on a journey, one takes a deep breath. Air offers inspiration and energy to begin, to plan, and to create. It also fuels us for motion and thought. The brain, muscles, and cells of the body need oxygen to perform the tasks of a living being. Without air, you would expire after about five minutes.

In the previous chapter, you explored soil aeration created by double digging and worm tunnels. Why is the air so important to the soil? Because oxygen is crucial for soil critters like bacteria and for plant roots. With oxygen, the roots can make sugars to feed the plant. The better aerated the soil, the more nutrients the roots can manufacture for its leaves or fruits. Air is also crucial to decaying processes; you turn your compost to invite in the air necessary to the bacteria and fungi that help decompose waste. Without air in compost, you get anaerobic decay, a smelly and sludgy mess.

Plants' leaves also need plenty of clean air, for they use carbon dioxide for photosynthesis, a plant technology that transforms solar energy into chemical-free energy. Through this process plants generate oxygen. Again, consider who is breathing: the plants or the animals? The dialectic answer recognizes breathing as a cycle of exchange, a great flowing of air through all life.

Air Meditation

This meditation will help you connect with the consciousness of air as you participate in the cycle of breath and spirit.

Go outside on a windy day. Take a deep breath and feel how your lungs interact with the breath of the world. Watch the breeze play with trees and grass, and observe how birds dance on the shifting winds. Feel the air on your skin, in your hair and clothes. Inhale the scent of wind. Listen to her sound as she dances with the trees, slips through a narrow spot, or slides around a corner. Taste her on your tongue. Now find a comfortable place to sit, and close your eyes. Feel the wind around you. Let your awareness extend beyond your own body and become part of the wind. Feel her lift you up, through the trees and over the land. How does it feel to be wind? What do you see, hear, and feel? When you are ready, open your eyes and feel the weight of your body on the ground. Stand up slowly and stretch to help return your consciousness fully to your body. What did you learn from the wind? Record your experience in your gardening journal. If you feel spacey afterwards, eat some food or drink a hot beverage to ground.

Revisit this meditation whenever you like, noticing how your awareness of "thin air" changes. A new relationship with the consciousness of air lends greater awareness to air magic in the garden, like planning and weather wisdom.

Planning the Garden

"From Nature's perspective, a garden is any environment that is initiated by humans, given its purpose, definition, and direction by humans, and maintained with the help of humans.... Nature looks at gardens as expressions of humans.... We consider an environment to be 'nature friendly' when humans understand that the elements used to create gardens are form and operate best under the laws of nature, and when humans have the best intentions of trying to understand what they understand these laws to be."

Nature, as communicated by Machaelle Small Wright[41]

Air magic includes mental energy like thinking and communicating, and you draw on the powers of air when you plan your garden. In the last chapter, you discovered where your land is shady or dry, and you discussed with the plants themselves how and where they wish to grow. In this chapter, you will identify your intentions for your space and work with the devas of the land to bring about your dreams. You will develop a plan for the whole space, incorporating sacred elements, spaces for play, and the flow of your everyday life into your organic garden.

To plan a sacred garden, be clear about your own intentions for the space—its purpose—while also listening to the nature of the land and what it wishes to express. While getting clear about your intentions can be fairly straightforward, listening to nature may be a skill you need to develop. Before you begin planning, take some time to explore your ability to communicate with nature.

Air magic is about communication, listening, and the quicksilver of the mind. To plan a garden, your air element must be in balance. Planning requires both the right and left aspects of the brain, creativity and logic. Therefore, when you plan a space, spend time not only mapping out where you wish to put your plants, water features, irrigation system, and so on, but also take time to simply sit in your space and hear what *it* wants to express. Each piece of land has its own flavor, its own spirit. Get to know the personality of your land, from the worms to the trees to the sky above. Listen from your heart as well as your head. By listening and offering your intentions, you can truly co-create a sacred space.

When I was planning a drought-resistant garden for a friend, we knew we wanted to remove the sod from her front yard and replace it with low-water perennials. I spent some time listening to the land, asking it what it would like to see and letting it know our intentions and limitations. We wanted to create a garden of beauty that would welcome visitors while protecting the home from intruders. We had a limited budget to work with and wanted to get the garden well on its way before my daughter was born that autumn. I wanted to create a space in the back for my friend's dog as well as for parties, but I wanted the yard to also be a retreat in the middle of the city.

A week after I tuned in to the garden and expressed our intentions, the men remodeling the house next door unintentionally caused some damage to my friend's side yard while replacing a water line. They offered to repair the path in whatever way she wished. My friend asked them if they would be willing to cart in bark mulch and remove the sod from her front yard; they were happy to do both at no charge. The timing was perfect, saved my friend time and money, and prepared the space for us to introduce drought-tolerant perennials. The exchange with the workers made everyone happy and assured that while my friend and her husband were away from the house it would be watched over, at least while the workers were there. By communicating with the land, we were able to easily achieve our goals.

Several months later, I waited to go into labor with my daughter. She was overdue by more than a week, and I felt a growing impatience. I wanted very much to trust the natural timing of her birth and was getting nervous about the possibility of being induced at 42 weeks. The day of the full moon, I sat in my yard and asked for guidance and patience. Movement out of the corner of my eye caught my attention; three hawks circled lazily in the hot autumn afternoon. They were several miles to the south, and I wondered what they found so interesting. As I watched, the three hawks drifted their spirals northward until they circled directly over my head. Craning my head back, I watched them head farther north until I couldn't see them anymore.

Later that day, my husband and I took a walk in a nearby park. We encountered a coyote and a turtle. Both wild animals looked directly at us, wary but unafraid. I took these three signs as encouragement: hawk is about being able to see the bigger picture, turtle teaches us about patience and right timing, and coyote encouraged me to be mindful of the calm before the storm of a newborn. My daughter was born naturally five days later.

Open your awareness to the nonhuman community around you, especially the creatures that call your garden home. Since you will be giving form to their home, it is crucial that you ask them for input. You will receive answers, either as signs and messages or in a more "psychic" way, just like you are having a conversation. Open to the possibility of an answer, and see what happens.

If listening to nonhumans is a new practice for you, here are a few techniques for learning to open up. First, identify the way in which you most easily receive nonverbal communication. Do you see, hear, or feel nonverbal or psychic information? Have you ever heard a voice, either aloud or in your mind (yet still been fully aware of "reality")? Or have you seen things out of the corner of your eye, or even head-on, like colors around a person's head? Or you may be kinesthetically intuitive, like I am; you may feel hunches and pulls in your body. Notice how you pick up things about people or surroundings, and record any experiences in your journal, no matter how insignificant. The best way to learn to trust your intuitive skills is to use them and to notice what happens as you learn to trust them. By recording your hunches and hits, you give yourself a place to process what happened as well as a record for later reference.

One way to become more comfortable with this form of communication is to calm the rational mind to allow intuitive information to surface. Art is one of the best tools for listening to the subconscious mind, where your intuition lives. Go outside with newsprint and crayons, pens, or paint. Get calm and centered. Ask your garden a question aloud, and then just start drawing. Try not to analyze what appears on the paper. You can also sing while you paint or draw, just letting the sounds come. Take moments to pause, and really feel the sensations in your body. Draw them, in whatever way arises naturally. Create as many drawings or paintings as you like, and do not worry about how the finished product looks. You may understand what arises as it pours on to the paper, or you may want to put your work aside and come back later to see what messages you received.

You can also use your journal as a listening tool. Again, go outside and become comfortable, calm, and centered. Ask a question of the garden, or focus your attention on a specific plant. Still your mind, and let any response simply arise. "Free write" in your journal, letting your pen nearly move on its own as it records your stream of consciousness.

Then take time to listen. Ask nature what it recommends in terms of plants, locations, and timing. Ask it questions, and allow time for the answers to arise. You can even tell it that you feel silly talking to "nature" but are willing to give it a try. I pick up answers with my body; Machaelle Small Wright, author of *Behaving as If the God in All Life Mattered*, uses kinesiology muscle testing and meditation to get her answers; for you, they may come in dreams. Pay attention also to synchronicities, the "coincidences" that let you know you are on the right path, like when I was visited by animals while waiting for my daughter's birth. Over time your ability to hear the nonhuman world will strengthen. For now, just have fun with it. Take some time to "tap in" as you go about planning the garden space.

Sacred Sister: Dorothy MacLean

writer & psychic

Author of *To Hear the Angels Sing,* Dorothy was one of the original founders of Findhorn, the garden community in northern Scotland. Against great financial and emotional hardship, she and Peter and Eileen Caddy vowed to live a life based completely on their inner guidance. They began growing vegetables for food in the sandy soils outside their trailer while meditating every day for guidance. It was during meditation that Dorothy began to receive instruction about how to work with the unseen powers of nature, the devas. She was informed that tuning into these forces would help with the garden.

She was told,

> "Begin this by thinking about the nature spirits, the higher

over-lighting nature spirits, and tune into them. That will be so unusual as to draw their interest here. They will be overjoyed to find some members of the human race eager for their help. That is the first step. By the higher nature spirits, I mean those such as the spirits of clouds, of rain, and of vegetables. The smaller individual nature spirits are under their jurisdiction."[42]

Over time, the garden at Findhorn became world-famous for its amazing vegetables, fruits, and flowers, grown even in sand and snow with help from the nature spirits. Though much of the support from devas came as direct communication, Dorothy also believes strongly that living in one's power is not about consulting the spirits or God like one would an oracle, but learning to listen to one's own inner guidance. Whether one wishes to grow a garden, buy a house, or follow her unknown life purpose, "If we approach our questions with the right attitude, we will find the right answer. When we need help, we can go inward and reconnect with our inner divinity, that feeling of joy and unconditional love, and see the external situation differently. When one is able to link with the unconditional love of God, everything on the outside changes," she told *Spirit of the Smokies* magazine in 1999.[43]

Dorothy now lives in the Pacific Northwest, traveling on occasion to teach workshops on communicating with the devas and other spirits. She has published *To Hear the Angels Sing, Choices of Love,* and *To Honor the Earth.* Her calm but bright presence reflects the deep wisdom she carries about the power each of us holds to create a world of unconditional love and cooperation.

The Evolving Plan

The first step in planning a garden is to identify your intentions. For what reason do you want to have a garden? To feed your family year-round? To have extra food to donate to a local shelter or food assistance program? To create a place where your children can play and learn about nature? Part of your plan should include the interconnections among plants, animals, insects, and the land itself, in addition to the people who will spend time in the garden. The elements of a garden can have multiple functions that address nonhuman and human needs. What plants and other elements will address multiple needs, like providing beauty, habitat, food for humans and animals, and shade in a sun-baked corner?

While you consider the many functions of your garden, observe what exists now and what needs the land has. Take time to just listen to the land itself. Observe using all of your senses, including subtle senses that can hear the voice of the land, the trees, and the animals. What does the garden itself want to express? How can you as the garden's creator work with the land to meet these goals?

When you have clarified your intentions, considered all uses of the land—human and nonhuman—and spent some time listening to the land, it's time to draw out a plan. This plan will develop over time and is only a guide. It need not be the work of a professional architect or planner. The plan is simply a place to explore ideas and to record them in a visual format. Remember that you are *creating* a garden. Do not be afraid to be creative and to have fun.

Include in your plan where you wish to put garden beds, pots, and trellises. Indicate how your plants will get water. Draw out paths, including already existing structures and plants. If you plan to create a new garden in a plot previously developed by someone else, like in a new house or in a plot in a community garden, incorporate the aspects that already exist. Recycle or reuse what was left behind, and consider your neighbors' plots' proximity to your own. How can you take advantage of what was done before, and how can you design your garden as a part of the larger whole?

Throw into your plan a few features you dream of but perhaps cannot afford right now, like a fountain or a stone wall. Let this plan be your dream to work toward as well as a practical guide to where you will dig a bed or plant a fruit tree. If you already have a garden, draw up a plan of what you wish to manifest over time as you build on your garden. When you put energy into a dream, even simple energy like drawing the stone wall of your imagination, you create a space for that dream to manifest.

Consider your favorite colors, stones, and images. Incorporate them through sculpture, a whimsical garden shed, and inviting pathways. You may wish to honor specific deities or incorporate the music of the planets in your garden. A garden designed for utilitarian purpose, such as feeding your family, should also include whimsy and magic—when it integrates fun as well as function you, your family, and the fairies will all want to spend more time in your magical garden.

Consider the four elements and spirit in planning your garden. How do each of the elements present themselves in your garden and interact with each other? How can you bring your own spirit into the land in conjunction with your allies? Discuss with the nature spirits aspects such as soil preparation, direction and size of plots, and modes of watering. Record all of the answers you receive in your garden journal.

Continue to listen to the land and your own heart, and let your garden plan evolve. As you get to know your land and climate better, develop a relationship with your gardening allies, and identify your needs as a gardener, your garden will grow and develop beyond anything you could once have imagined.

GODDESS

Feng-Po

The goddess of air and storms, Feng-Po carries a great bag over her shoulder in which she keeps the winds. She rides a tiger along a path of clouds, flinging open her magic bag and telling the winds where to go.

Hear her laughter in the rustle of the trees, and know her delight in the power of a hurricane.

On calm days, we know Feng-Po has captured the winds in her bag, waiting for the right time to release them and stir up a storm.[44]

Weather

Since 1792 gardeners have turned to *The Old Farmer's Almanac* for information about the weather, gardening, moon cycles, and more. The first author, Robert B. Thomas, came up with a special formula for determining the weather, said to be 80 percent accurate. His system even included some uncanny and accurate predictions like a great snowstorm in July of 1816. Today one can find weather predictions not only in this and other almanacs, but also on the Internet and the Weather Channel. However, *The Old Farmer's Almanac* is the only publication in America making day-to-day forecasts eighteen months ahead of time. They do so using very witchy sources: the sun and the moon.[45]

Weather-predicting sources are invaluable, but every gardener should learn to sense weather patterns on their own. Knowing when to plant tomatoes or harvest the last broccoli simply by checking in with the wind, sun, and nature devas is one of the marks of a true garden goddess.

To develop your own innate weather sense, pay attention to the weather every day. Note the location of the moon and the stars. Observe the sunrise. Learn to smell rain and the changing seasons. Before you plant or harvest, check in with the spirits of the land to see if this is a good time. Take their advice. In my impatience for summer one year, I planted tomatoes three weeks too early, despite the tomato deva suggesting I wait. I had to pull the poor things up and replace them a month later.

At times you may wish to encourage the weather toward

a certain direction, inviting rain or asking humbly for a hailstorm to spare your chard. It is said that priestesses of Isis could control the weather by braiding or unbinding their hair, and Native shamans perform yearly rain dances to ensure sufficient moisture for the tribe's crops. Take care, though, for weather magic is a delicate matter. My husband called for rain to quench our dry Colorado land the week before our wedding. It rained for four days straight, clearing up only for our ceremony. We had sixty people huddled in our small house, unable to go out in the yard for fear of catching cold in June in normally hot, arid Colorado. Be careful what you ask for, and keep in mind that what we want right now for our plot of land may not be in the greater interest of the rest of the community or the planet.

Weather is one of Gaia's magics that puts us humans in our place. We can beg her for moisture or sunlight to bless our gardens in whatever element our climate lacks and call in storms or droughts if we're not careful. Because there are so many of us humans in industrialized nations, we have affected weather patterns immensely by pumping greenhouse gases into the atmosphere at levels high enough to impact air flow, freezing levels, and the melting of glaciers. As our careless attitudes bring greater imbalance to the planet, Gaia unleashes more violent weather systems to balance our folly.

Climate shifts like these are already well underway and no longer what-if scenarios for the future. It is time we speak openly about the power of weather and how it is a relationship with the human community, not just an "act of God." We need to accept that we have changed the planet, and we need to come up with plans for how to live on a different Earth than our ancestors were used to. We need to do this in community, a community that includes the energy of air and the spirits of the weather.

Use your powers of weather witching by communicating directly with the elements to ask how you can help evolve the human relationship with the planet's climate. Hold healing rituals in your garden, offering thanks for the gifts of the earth. Burn lavender incense as a gift to the air, and hang wind chimes anointed with honey (just enough without making them sticky!) to give honor to the winged ones. Draw on the wisdom of other cultures, especially indigenous practices, to determine what plants grow best under extreme weather conditions. Research local indigenous plants, and speak to elders about how they learned to garden with the land. If your land needs to be in a time of drought or massive storms to bring balance, accept the wisdom of the planet, even if your own garden grows poorly that year. Remember that we live in community with nonhumans like birds and rivers, and we need to remember them in challenging weather as well. When we share our resources with them, like water and food, we establish a strength that will serve us in return when we need it.

Gardening with the Planets

Everything in the universe is vibration, and vibrations vibrate each other. All things resonate together in a symphony too vast for the human mind to fully grasp. One being hums its own frequency, and another picks up that hum, adding its unique tones to the mix. Multiply this exchange by near infinity and you have a uni-verse—one song.

This song is made up of an infinite number of resonances, from the minute to the vast. What we call a thing or a being is actually a community of beings within a larger community, like our own bodies. We are trillions of cells breathing and metabolizing. Within each cell live the mitochondria, the "powerhouses" of the cell, organelles that millions of years ago were distinct microscopic creatures. Mitochondria have their own DNA, and it is their life process that makes it possible for us to live. Within our intestines and on our skin live other distinct but interrelated beings, a variety of bacteria. We are not just one individual, but a community. In turn, we exist as a part of a larger web.

This web includes not just the living Earth but the solar system and the galaxy. The planets contribute in a very real way to our existence, just as we support mitochondria. The moon, for instance, keeps Earth on a fairly regular rotation by tugging on us with her gravitational pull. Without the moon, Earth would wobble too greatly on her axis to support consistent climates and, therefore, life as we know it. The gravitational pull of the larger planets like Saturn also protects us, by diverting meteors from pummeling Earth.

Sacred gardening is about tuning in to the many different beings singing together to create the uni-verse. Your garden is one piece of the great song, one weave in the tapestry of all things. When you tug on the strands of this weave, you interact with everything, from the winds to the "distant" planet Uranus. You can begin to attune to this dance by studying the frequencies of the planets and consciously shaping those frequencies in your garden by setting up theme gardens or altars using some of the following ideas. The gems and stones suggested are not intended as mechanistic spellmaking, but as ways to attune the gardener's consciousness and intention with the body of each celestial body. As with all of the magical gardening techniques suggested in this book, the real magic is attuning your spirit and intention with the holon of the universe by gaining a deeper awareness of its parts.

The Sun

According to Mayan teachings, the sun is the resonator through which we receive galactic information via light quanta.[46] You can learn much and grow immensely by listening to our closest star through meditation in a sun garden. In chapter 3: Fire, we will explore the sun further.

In your sun listening space, include the colors gold and yellow. Gold coins, sun shapes, golden orbs or bowls, and sun catchers can help you charge the space with sun energy. Sprinkle the land with clove and cinnamon oil, spices of the sun. Include statues of the hawk, lion, fire dragon, or phoenix. Plant any of the following to draw in sun energy:

- Ash, bay, bromeliad, carnation, cedar, chamomile, chicory, chrysanthemum, citrus, goldenseal, heliotrope, juniper, lovage, marigold, oak, olive, peony, rosemary, rowan, rue, St. John's wort, sunflower, and witch hazel.[47]

The Moon

The moon goddess dances in natural cycles of three and thirteen. She moves through the trinity of maiden, mother, and crone every twenty-eight days, making a year thirteen moons long. The Incas, Mayans, ancient Egyptians, and Lakotas use a twenty-eight day calendar, which is more earth- and moon-based than our solar calendar. Our bodies often naturally follow this calendar, and by consciously aligning with it you can improve your fertility, intuition, and compassion.

As Dr. Christiane Northrup, MD, writes in *Women's Bodies, Women's Wisdom,*

> Scientific research has documented that the moon rules the flow of fluids...and affects the unconscious mind and dreams. The timing of the menstrual cycle, the fertility cycle, and labor also follows the moon-dominated tides of the ocean....Since our culture generally appreciates only what we can understand rationally, many women tend to block at every opportunity the flow of unconscious 'lunar' information that comes to them premenstrually or during their menstrual cycle....When we routinely block the information that is coming to us in the second half of our menstrual cycles (the dark moon time), it has no choice but to come back as PMS or menopausal madness, in the same way that other feelings or bodily symptoms, if ignored, often result in illness.[48]

By opening to our own lunar cycle and information, we live in greater balance and health. Plant a moon garden to focus your own moon energy.

A garden dedicated to the moon includes silver and white plants and a reflective surface like a bird bath or round mirror placed flat on the earth. Include flowers of lavender, blue, and white. Goddesses associated with the moon include Isis, Diana, Luna, and Selena—as well as thousands more from other cultures—and, in the moon's dark phase, Hecate or Proserpine the Crone; call in these forces with statues, epitaphs, or simple intention. Decorate your space with moonstones and pearls (real or costume). Also include the following moon plants:

- Camellia, chickweed, cucumber, grape, pea, pear, jasmine, poppy, and wintergreen.[49]

Mercury

Mercury is the messenger of the gods; his quicksilver mind brings us new ways of seeing and being. He helps us make decisions and stick to them, as well as respond to opportunities with alacrity and grace. His energies tonify the nervous system, but only when it has support from more grounded energies like the earth. Too much Mercury without enough earth can leave a person wired and anxious—like when you've been talking on the phone too long. Call on Mercury while grounding in the earth to help you achieve the right balance.

To honor Mercury in the garden, include any of the following plants:

- Almond, aspen, bean, celery, clover, dill, fennel, fern, horehound, lavender, lemongrass, lemon verbena, lily of the valley, marjoram, mint, parsley, peppermint, and summer savory.[50]

Venus

To honor Venus, include a copper bowl (place it on a stone, for copper can poison soil bacteria and animals) and images of cats or doves in your garden. She is the Lady of Love, so include in your Venus shrine images or objects that inspire romance. You may wish to place your Venus garden a little off the beaten path, away from neighbors' eyes, and include a bed of moss and violets for outdoor lovemaking. Incorporate any of the following plants:

- African violets, alder, alfalfa (which can be grown as a ground cover or grown tall and cut for compost), apple, bachelor buttons, birch, blackberry, bleeding heart, burdock, catnip, cherry, corn, crocus, daffodil, daisy, feverfew, foxglove, geranium, goldenrod, heather, hyacinth, Indian paintbrush, iris, larkspur, lilac, and willow.[51]

Mars

The warrior, Mars gives us courage to face life's challenges. There are many kinds of warriorship, from hate-filled vengeance to strong-hearted support of people and issues we hold dear. Chögyam Trungpa Rinpoche wrote, "The key to warriorship…is not being afraid of who you are."[52] Mars is about action and self-assertiveness. He also teaches us about aggression, which is a natural human drive we must learn to be in relationship with so that we do not self-destruct or harm others. Mars tones the immune system, our body's defense mechanism.

He lends us strength and endurance when we need it.

To honor Mars in your garden, plant any of the following:

- Basil, broom, cactus, carrot, chives and onions, cilantro, garlic, hawthorn, honeysuckle, mustard, nettles, pennyroyal, pine, snapdragon, thistle, and woodruff.[53]

Jupiter

Jupiter carries the power of storms, water, and fatherhood, and teaches us about nourishment and judgment. He can be called on to help you make the most nourishing decisions for your life. He calms and relaxes without sedation.

His colors are blue and purple; include stones such as lapis, turquoise, and amethyst in your Jupiter garden. Plant cedars, pines, oaks, and firs, and include the following herbs and flowers:

- Borage, carnation, clover, dandelion, dock, echinacea, honeysuckle, hyssop, Jupiter's beard, and sage.[54]

Saturn

We celebrate Christmas on December 25 because of the ancient holiday of Saturnalia, when the Romans marked the winter solstice. This was a time of merry-making and gift giving, and of celebrating Saturn, the god of agriculture. Saturn is also the god of time, who heralds in the new solar year.

Saturn provides us with structure, patience, and stability. He teaches us there is a time for everything, and through discipline and inner power, you will create your life's dreams.

To honor Saturn in your garden, include black and

indigo stones like onyx and jet. Include the following plants:

- Amaranth, beet, comfrey, cypress, datura, hemlock, hemp, ivy, lobelia, morning glory, mullein, quince, and yew.[55]

Neptune

The god of the deep teaches you about your own watery, emotional core. To learn more about your dreams or psychic impressions, call on Neptune to guide you through the shifting shadows of the Dreamtime. He will rock your cerebral spinal fluid to the tune of the ancient Mother, carrying you deep into a trance state. Here, in the watery depths, you can reconnect with compassion and a connection with all beings.

Plants that grow out in all directions and those associated with the sea call in Neptune. These include:

- coleus, creeping succulents, jasmine, morning glory, strawberry, and water lilies.[56]

Uranus

Aquarian Uranus brings electrical change. He is the Greek god of the sky and heavens, and is married to Gaia, Mother Earth. He can be eccentric, awakening the lightning bolt of creativity or chaos. He can help heal scar tissue and calculus, like kidney stones or bone spurs, by bringing in a jolt of life that breaks up old, stubborn ways. Many healers I have known were Aquarian.

Honor him in your garden with pokeweed (which can cause irritation, so handle with care), bryony, and plants with blue leaves like hosta or bluish grasses. Include images of lightning or electricity. You may want to set up your Uranus garden next to an electric pole or switch box, and ask him to watch over your home's energy.

Pluto

Pluto was recently determined to be a dwarf planet, but since for so long it has been included in alchemical and astrological lore, I will include it here. A powerful healing ally, Pluto will guide you through dark times and places. A god of transformation, death, and rebirth, Pluto helps those who face major changes like divorce or loss. He helps you shed old aspects of yourself that no longer serve you. At times we must all enter the cave of transmutation, and Pluto can gently, if firmly, guide you through the darkness. Tread with care, for he can use tough love to nudge you along your path.

To call on Pluto in the garden, choose bulbs and deep-rooted plants. Plant the following:

- Acacia, 'Black Barlow' columbine, black viola and pansy, coneflower, fireweed, larkspur, and male fern.[57]

Chiron

Located in 1977, Chiron follows an irregular orbit between Uranus and Saturn. Chiron follows a different drummer and brings an end to suffering. In mythology, he was a centaur who was accidentally wounded by his friend Hercules. He begged Zeus to let him die, for centaurs are immortal and his wound could not kill him. Zeus allowed him to die and placed him in the stars to guide us on our own quests for healing and inner wisdom.

A garden for Chiron would include unique and strange

plants as well as those you use for healing. Grow lavender, marigolds, and comfrey for use in salves. Cornflowers and bachelor buttons, which have the Latin name of *Centaurea*, were named for Chiron, who used the blue flowers for healing wounds.[58] Research which *Centaurea* species grow best in your area, and plant them in honor of Chiron.

Sedna

In 2003, astronomers near San Diego discovered a small planet orbiting the sun far beyond Pluto. Because of her frigid temperatures and distant home, they named her Sedna for the Inuit sea goddess who lives at the bottom of the northern seas. This creation goddess was betrayed by her father; when he threw her into the sea in fear of her Raven Spirit husband, she tried to crawl back in the boat. Her father cut off her fingers with his ice axe, and she sank to the depths of the ocean. Her fingers became creatures of the sea, and she became the cold Sea Queen. The Inuits do not worship Sedna, but instead fear and respect her, as befits the sea.[59]

To honor Sedna in the garden, include sealike plants like aloes, green or blue grasses, and beaded succulents. Images of the sea, sea mammals, and shells also honor this goddess. The planet is a balance of fire and ice energy, so ruddy-colored stones placed in a cool, dark corner of the yard will conjure up her teachings about loss, renewal, and compassion.

GODDESS

Seshat

The Egyptian star goddess Seshat blesses us with clear communication. She embodies the powers of the sky, including communication and beginnings.

Her name means "female scribe," and she is mistress of the house of books and the minister of time. As the great accountant, she remembers all since the very beginning. She creates the ever-unfolding world using sacred geometry, and her magic wand featuring a seven-pointed star represents the source of all creative ideas.[60]

When planning your garden, call on Seshat for her creative guidance. She will watch over the land, remembering each moment as it unfolds, blessing you with the powers of the air.

Air Ally: Bee

Bee can teach us much about community and about striving for our goals. She works hard for her sisters and for her queen, and in return she depends on them for sustenance, guidance, and community. "Bee knows the value of organization, of paying homage to the Goddess and the sun, and of working hard," write Philip and Stephanie Carr-Gomm in *The Druid Animal Oracle*.[61] A bee is dedicated to her community, and in doing her work she serves the greater ecosystem.

Aphrodite's high priestess at the honeycomb-shrine of Mount Eryx was named the Melissa, which means "queen bee." It was believed that Aphrodite and her sacred bees manufactured a sacred elixir of life, a combination of menstrual blood and honey. This elixir kept the gods alive.[62]

Melissa officinalis is the Latin name for bee balm, part of the order Labiate, the mints. *Labiate* means "lipped." This order of plants, which includes mint, catnip, and sage, has tubular petals divided into two unequal parts, one projecting over the other like the lips of the mouth. The order that bees, wasps, and ants belong to is called *hymenoptera*, meaning "veil-winged." *Hymen* means "veil," and in old temples devoted to the Goddess, a veil known as a hymen hid the inner sanctum. The same is true in a maiden who has not yet engaged in intercourse or otherwise broken her yoni's veil. What a sacred gift is honey, then, the union of hymenoptera and labiate: a sexy gift from the kiss of the Goddess.

A bee makes honey by collecting nectar as a carbohydrate source, mixing it with an enzyme that converts sucrose to glucose or fructose and depositing it in the hive where her sisters evaporate out any moisture by fanning their wings over the honey. Bees make honey as a food source for the winter, but they make more than enough for the hive, allowing us humans and other animals to share in the bounty. To make a pound of honey, a bee flies a distance equal to more than two times around the world, visiting more than two million flowers.[63] A honeybee visits only one type of flower, making her an invaluable pollinator.

It is estimated that in the United States bees pollinate one quarter of all fruits grown for human consumption. By doing so, they do between $10 and $14 billion worth of work, and their contribution affects the prices of common foods like almonds, cherries, and apples.[64] In addition to fruits and vegetables consumed by humans, bees pollinate many garden and wild flowers, contributing to the greater ecosystem and to the planet's beauty.[65]

Some bees gather nectar while others collect pollen, and others of the community stay back at the hive to raise young or serve the queen. The pollen gatherers get pollen caught in the hairs on their foraging bodies and carry it to the next flower. When they get too dusty, they stop to groom themselves, mixing their saliva with pollen and depositing it on their pollen basket to be saved for food. Pollen is very high in protein, containing five to seven times more than beef by weight.[66] Pollen that has been mixed with saliva is no longer available for plant pollination and is used only as a nutritious food source for the hive. It can also be used as a health supplement for humans; bee pollen or royal bee jelly is a complete food source, containing amino acids, vitamins, minerals, and hormones. It can be used as a cure for any deficiency caused by an unbalanced diet and is a powerful immunity builder. Pollen and honey can help protect us against food-born pathogens, increase healthy blood cells, reduce cholesterol, and provide relief from premenstrual and menopausal complications, asthma, and allergies (although some people are allergic to bee pollen—taste only a few grains at first to see if you have a reaction). Pollen, royal jelly, and honey also contain high levels of antioxidants, and are antimicrobial and antiseptic.[67] It takes a lot of work for a bee to collect one grain of bee pollen, so if you consume this gift, do so in small amounts and with great respect.

Honey has been used for thousands of years as an embalming fluid, for it holds preserving qualities. You can benefit from its preserving and protecting qualities while still alive. Make a lovely and powerful herbal remedy by soaking an herbal ally like dandelion or lavender in honey for a moon cycle or more. Eat it by the teaspoonful, pour it in your bath, and rub it into your skin.

In addition to offering us the sweetness of honey, bees are masters of nonverbal communication, and to explain to their sisters where a good source of nectar or pollen may be found, they perform a complex dance. Using circles, figure-eights, and butt waggles, a worker bee describes to her hive sisters how to get to a patch of prime flowers. They don't only work hard to support their community, however; they also take time to relax, grooming each other and simply kicking back.

Bees are severely threatened today due to habitat loss, pesticide use, and invasive mites. To help these allies recover, stop all use of pesticides and encourage others to do the same by buying organic fruits, flowers, and nuts. If you have a large field, leave a cover crop of clover or simply allow the land to go fallow when not planted. This will provide wild bees with nesting habitat.

To attune with the bee goddess Melissa, try a cup of the following tea, from Rosemary Gladstar's *Family Herbal:*

Melissa Tea Blend

- 3 parts lemon balm
- 1 part borage flowers and leaves
- 1 part chamomile
- 1 part lemon verbena
- 1 part St. John's wort

Combine herbs, put in a jar, and pour boiling water over them (about one cup herb mixture to one pint water, or more herbs to make it stronger). Cover and let sit for at least twenty minutes. Strain and drink. Good with honey and lemon; makes a great iced tea, too.[68]

GODDESS

Melissa

Melissa is the bee goddess, high priestess of Aphrodite. She brings her heavenly honey to heal our bodies and hearts. Her sting is intense, reminding us painfully to become more present to our surroundings—pay attention!—yet healing; bee stings can help heal arthritis and multiple sclerosis.

Melissa officinalis, commonly known as lemon balm or bee balm, is calming and tonifying.

Drink melissa tea to attune with this sweet but powerful goddess and to find renewed energy (see recipe, page 89).

The Birds and the Bees

The reproductive process of flowers depends heavily on air magic, be it by winged creature or wind. Plants that produce nectar are fertilized by insects and birds, including bees, flies, beetles, gnats, and hummingbirds. Those plants that do not produce nectar are wind pollinated, except for a few rather stinky flowers that attract flies (and a few self-pollinating flowers that often still rely on a nudge of wind). As much as sixty to seventy percent of all plants are pollinated by insects, and the bee is the predominant but not sole pollinator in most northern areas.

Of course this is where the phrase "the birds and the bees" comes from: all that pollinating! Unlike our culture's image of sex as shameful and dirty, or at least private, the planet includes sex as a simple part of her growth and development. In the pagan calendar, there is a holiday devoted to pollination and sexual reproduction: Beltane or May Day. As Phyllis Curott writes, Beltane celebrates when "the Goddess and God join in love and the Earth blossoms in Ecstasy."[69] Ecstatic pollination is deeply sacred to the Goddess, and each burrowing bee, unfolding bud, and juicy fruit is offered as a celebration of the gift of life and love granted us. On Beltane and throughout the year, say a prayer of thanks to the pollinators. Join efforts to protect bats and bees, and help restore wild habitats for our friends to give back some of what they have gifted us.

Air Ally: Bird

Every gardener knows the joy of a chorus of chattering birds in her trees. Dainty red-headed house finches twitter and dart about in their spring mating rituals. At dusk, robins chirp and call to their friends as they scavenge for worms and bugs in the grass. Overhead circles a graceful hawk against the blue of a summer sky. The garden is full of bird magic.

Approximately 870 species of birds call the lower 48 states of the U.S. home, so to list the magic of each species would take a separate tome all to itself. Let us look at some of the shared traits of these varied and delightful creatures of air.

Birds evolved from a group of small bipedal dinosaurs. Over time their scales developed into feathers, allowing them to take long glides. About a hundred million years ago, they evolved into a form fairly similar to the modern bird, including being warm blooded (humans, on the other hand, resembled our modern form only about forty thousand years ago). Birds have been fluttering about the field, shore, and garden for 99,960,000 years longer than we have. They can, therefore, teach us something about the garden's story.

Birds are the sowers, having planted seeds in the earth since the beginning of their evolution. Birds co-evolved with fruit-bearing plants in an I'll-feed-you-if-you-spread-me relationship. When we plant a seed in the ground or save seed from manure plants, we participate in an ancient dance. Certainly the first humans who discovered agriculture watched birds eat seeds and fruit and learned from them what is edible and how to create new edible plants from seed.

Birds also provide great fertilizer as they spread seed, a fact humans also discovered thousands of years ago. Guano, composted bird or bat droppings amassed over hundreds of years, was widely used as a fertilizer in pre-Spanish Latin America and became an important trade commodity in the nineteenth century. Like all fertilizers made from excrement, it is high in nitrogen and phosphorus. Guano from Peru was mined from fish-eating birds and therefore contained minerals and nutrients from the sea as well.

Today, poultry manure is a major trade commodity in the United States. Some poultry farms carefully manage the amount of phosphorus and nitrogen in the birds' feed with the nutrient value of their droppings in mind. Too much nitrogen and phosphorus in manure turns into runoff and a source of ground-water pollution, so more tightly managing the content of chicken manure improves the environment while being good for business.

Over one fifth of all bird species are at risk for extinction, mostly due to habitat destruction. Songbirds provide us with a sort of barometer for the state of the environment: they are all canaries in the mine of the world. You can help birds by learning which species are threatened or endangered in your area and participating in habitat conservation, by not using pesticides or chemicals on other avian food sources and by donating money to international conservation programs.

A crucial part of saving birds and other threatened species is to raise our children with respect for the natural world. Set up a bird-watching station in your yard, raising feeders more than six feet off the ground to keep birds safe from cats. Participate in local bird counts with your children or organize a birding club for children in your area. If you are raising your children with an awareness of energy and magic, include bird healing rituals in your family practices. Teach them about the magic of individual birds as well.

Bird magic is about planting and fertilizing, but their power includes the energy of the soul as well. Barbara Walker, in *The Women's Encyclopedia of Myths and Secrets,* writes, "Because birds traveled freely between the earthly and heavenly realms, they were everywhere regarded as angelic messengers, givers of omens, possessors of occult secrets, as well as soul-carriers."[70] The Egyptians carved openings in the pyramids to allow one's soul in the form of a hawk to fly freely between the body and the heavens. Well known today is the myth of the stork, the great bird that brings a new soul to its earthly home. The phoenix, a brightly colored mythological bird, represents rebirth and literally rising from the ashes. Call on Bird during times of transition and metamorphosis.

The birds in our garden can carry our wishes for a vibrant garden to the realm of the fey. They can be oracles of both things unseen and the weather. Magpies and ravens have long been regarded as oracles by the Greeks and Native Americans.

Here are some of the more common birds in North America and their energies.[71]

Blackbird: Teaches us about enchantment; urges us to follow our spiritual path to our inner knowing.

Crane: Offers secret knowledge, patience, and longevity; helps us to persevere and focus; guides us into or through the Underworld.

Crow: Teaches about universal sacred laws. The Master of Illusion teaches us also about shapeshifting and the illusion of "reality." Omen of change, calling to integrity.

Eagle: A symbol of intelligence, renewal, courage, and the Great Spirit. Helps us rejuvenate and approach situations with clarity. Associated with the sun and all its bright power.

Goose: A bird of vigilance, parenthood, and productive power; teaches us about staying both spiritual and grounded while committed to a family or cause.

Grouse: Teaches us the sacred spiral dance by moving through the world with intention and beauty.

Hawk: Nobility, recollection, cleansing; seeing your life in perspective; the messenger that helps you see the truth.

Hummingbird: Joy. Opens the heart, teaches us about new directions and non-duality.

Owl: Detachment, wisdom, change, clairvoyance, magic. Sacred to Athena, speaker of truth.

Raven: Healing, initiation, protection; grants the gift of prophecy. Change in consciousness, magic. Was the first bird Noah released from his ark, representing rebirth.

Swan: Soul, love, beauty, grace; can travel to the Otherworld. Sings of altered states, healing, and transformation.

Turkey: A bird of sacrifice and the giveaway—a Native American tradition of sacred giving. Models compassionate giving and knowledge that the Great Spirit lives in everyone.

Wren: Humility, cunning. Small is beautiful, gentle wit is powerful.

To connect with bird energy and their powers of rebirth, new vision, courage, and beauty, greet each bird with respect as she enters your yard. Even carrion birds and invasive birds like the starling teach us about the laws of the universe and the compassion of the earth. Listen as they communicate with each other, and know that powerful air magic is present. Remember also that birds exist not just for us humans but on their own terms, and respect them in their natural habitat.

GODDESS

Selene

THE GODDESS OF the full moon, Selene is also known as Semele, Zemelo, and Cybelle. The full moon radiates the plenitude of lover, bride, and mother. She blesses all nocturnal beings, the crickets and bats and night-blooming flowers.

To call her blessings upon your garden, place a gold or silver glass globe next to white flowers.

Plant rose, bluebell, and nicotiana in her honor, and she will help your garden grow with fullness and vigor.

Air Ally: Bat

Many people fear bats for their nocturnal leatheriness and fangs, but these gentle and fascinating creatures offer great wisdom and power to the planet. They keep our insect populations down to a dull roar, and they pollinate night-blooming flowers, including many popular fruits. They provide invaluable nutrients to the earth with their guano, which may also be able to help clean industrial pollution out of lakes and streams.[72]

Bats have a bad reputation as rabies carriers, vampires, and "flying rodents," a sad misunderstanding of these amazing creatures. The risk of rabies from bats is actually extremely low, and they are more than happy to stay quite literally out of our hair. Without bats' contribution as pollinators, we would not have mangos, avocados, tequila, cloves, or even tropical rain forests. Bats are so important as pollinators, they are known as a keystone species; should they go extinct or their populations diminish drastically, many other plant and animal species would be adversely affected.[73] Bats are extremely important members of our community.

There are over 950 known species of bats on the planet, including 150 mega bats and 800 species of *Microcheroptera,* or micro bats. Mega bats live in the tropics—without them, rainforests would not be able to survive—and may be neurologically related to primates. These tropical bats can grow up to a six-foot wingspan. Micro bats, those swooping overhead at night in northern climates, live throughout the planet, except in the most extreme conditions. Bats are mammals, not rodents. Their teeth are generally too small to bite a human, and even vampire bats (found in the tropics) do not suck blood. They simply form a tiny incision and lap at the nutrient-rich flow.

Bats have more to fear from us than we from bats. They are the most endangered land mammals in North America. Cave vandalism, pollution, and habitat destruction have drastically reduced their numbers. To help protect bats, stay out of caves. Hang a bat house in a high, unobstructed area like a telephone pole (check with local animal experts for suggestions and requirements). Don't use pesticides or harsh chemicals, which not only poison bugs and weeds but the bats further down the food chain. Recent research demonstrates that bats thrive in organic garden spaces, drawn to the healthy abundance of insects.[74]

Bats cannot take off like birds but must fall from a height. Look for them just after dusk at the edges of the trees, fluttering about in search of dinner. Listen to their echolocation, a clicking sound that helps them "see" in the dark. Call on Bat if you need clarity in the dark or help in moving through a time of change and rebirth.

Bats teach about reincarnation and rebirth, as they emerge nightly from the Goddess' womb. They also teach us about shamanic death, the ending of old ways and the initiation into new powers. A few days before our wedding, my husband and I were greeted by a bat clinging to the screen on the window outside our breakfast table. After staring at us with great curiosity and a bit of fear, she dove away and took flight into the nearby trees. We smiled at each other, knowing that in a few days we would surrender our nonmarried selves to the past. The next time I saw a bat close up was only weeks before finding a publisher for this book. Never underestimate the power of Bat.

Air Ally: Sylphs

The air elemental, sylphs are often depicted much the way you might think of a fairy, dancing lightly on the wind with shimmery wings. They are one of the manifestations of air consciousness and can help you with inspiration if you offer them your respect and honor. These beings are attracted by oils and incense and will announce their presence with a scented breeze.

Sylphs and their cousins the zephyrs will help you imagine your dream garden. They will lend you herbal knowledge and inspire your work with the land. They help you develop psychic abilities and develop new ideas. The truth and things lost will be revealed with their help.

Images of fairies and angels in your garden will let these elementals know they are honored and welcome.

Air Ally: Dragonfly

Dragonflies have been around for over three hundred million years, longer than dinosaurs and birds.[75] These beautiful insects bridge water and air, for in a larval stage they develop in water. To invite dragonflies into your yard, offer a small pond for their larva. Include a pump and filter to provide clean, aerated water and discourage mosquitoes. Include a few aquatic plants in which the adults can lay their eggs, but make sure at least some of the water is free of plants, including algae, and in sunlight. The larva will live in your pond for a year or more, climb up a plant stem to shed their nymph's exoskeleton, and become an adult. It will live as an adult for a few weeks.

As babies, larval dragonflies feed on other aquatic insects and even small fish. As adults, they eat mosquitoes and other insects. In both their larval and adult phases, they provide a valuable food source for larger carnivores, such as fish, frogs, and birds.

Dragonfly in the garden not only fills a valuable niche in the food-web, it gives a powerful lesson in illusion. *The Medicine Cards* read:

> Dragonfly medicine is of the dreamtime and the illusionary façade we accept as physical reality. The iridescence of Dragonfly's wings reminds us of colors not found in our everyday experience. Dragonfly's shifting of color, energy, form, and movement explodes into the mind of the observer, bringing vague memories of a time or place where magic reigned.[76]

Dragonfly helps you enter the sacred dimensions of the garden. Magic reigns not in a lost dreamtime but in the here and now, and dragonfly can help us reconnect with this shifting but present space. As she has been around so very long, she can teach you about Deep Time and bring you outside your limiting beliefs about chronos. She also teaches about transformation and patience: a dragonfly can spend up to five years in her larval stage before she undergoes a rebirth into an adult, teaching you that sometimes it just takes time to grow into the shimmering being you know yourself to be.

GODDESS

Aurora

WE MEET ROSY Eos or Aurora in the clear rays of dawn. A Greek goddess whose name means "light," she rides into each morning on Pegasus the winged horse or in a purple and golden chariot.

To bring her blessing on your garden and to welcome new light into your life, burn a rose-colored candle anointed with morning dew at dawn on the spring equinox. Sing a soft song of morning light to welcome her gifts into your life.

Sister Jose Hobday, Native American elder and Franciscan Sister, teaches a simple dawn ritual. Upon awaking, go outside and take three intentional steps. With the first, step into the day. On the second, step into yourself; and on the third, step into the unknown that your day will bring. Give thanks to Aurora for the blessing of each new day.[77]

AIR ALLY: BUTTERFLY

These lovely insects teach us about transformation. As you pass through cyclical transformations in your life, from a larval stage to pupal stage to your emergence as a winged creature, you can turn to butterfly for guidance and encouragement.

An air being, Butterfly teaches about clarity and community; air is about being individual and unique yet connected with all things, for each of us breathes our own breath from the collective breath of the planet. Butterfly too shares this collective breath as she dances from flower to flower.

As she flutters about her day, the butterfly helps to fertilize the flowers she encounters and also provides food for insects and birds. She teaches about interdependence, the connection of all things.

Butterflies possess a fine sense of smell and can detect their favorite flowers from miles away. To attract butterflies into your garden, plant native flowering plants and vines. Be sure to include plants for butterfly larvae as well as adult food. Set up a birdbath, for butterflies need a constant supply of moisture. Refresh the water in your butterfly bath regularly to prevent mosquito infestations.

There are hundreds of butterfly varieties, so if you wish to attract a certain species, research its flowers of choice. To learn more about which butterflies live in your area and which plants they prefer, visit www.butterflies.com, or visit your library for books on local species.

Air Magic: Creating a Garden Community

Air teaches about communication and community. In Middle French, *commune* meant "free city, group of citizens." Many of today's teachers of democracy urge us not to wait for those in political power to provide for us what we desire, but to go out and create it ourselves as free citizens. Gardens provide a powerful focal point for community building that can lead to local change you might never have dreamed possible. As St. Francis of Assisi said, "Start by doing what's necessary, then what's possible, and suddenly you are doing the impossible."[78]

In our modern society, much of our "community" is invisible and removed from our everyday awareness. Consider when you sit down to a meal all that went into getting this food to your table: the soil and water, pollinators, farmers, truck drivers, oil workers that extracted the petroleum to fuel the tractors and trucks, the produce worker, the animals and plants in the meal, and so on. Being removed from this community ignores the interdependence of all beings. We can no longer afford the luxury of this ignorance.

Recognizing interdependence not only gets us in touch with reality, it provides key tools for survival in a shifting world. We are already seeing how healthful food, fresh water, affordable services, and elder care, to name but a few necessities, are harder to find in a culture that values money over life. Within a supportive community, these resources are commonplace or can be developed as needs arise. By strengthening community through the garden, you return yourself and your people to Life.

The garden can be used as a tool to heal communities and strengthen those who live there. One study examined the relationship between gardening, self-efficacy, and nutrition among seniors. Raised garden boxes were provided to the study's participants, who received weekly home visits and attended monthly meetings on nutrition and gardening. The study showed that gardening with support improved the elders' attitudes and dietary behaviors.[79] Another study through the University of California at Davis found the same to be true of children who garden. Young people who worked in a garden throughout the school year were significantly more willing to try new vegetables than children who did not garden.[80] This translates into future savings in health care for obesity, heart disease, and immune problems—not to mention the quality of a child's life.

One simple way to build community through gardening is to bring your garden out of the back yard and put it in front of your house. While you tend the plants or build an altar to the Goddess, neighbors will stop to say hello, ask questions, and give praise. You can offer them a taste of your latest harvest, give them a tour, and ask them about their own gardening practices. You never know where this exchange might grow.

Invite your neighbors, young and old, into your garden. Show them what you grow and why, and share the stories of your triumphs and challenges. You might even invite them to grow a few things in your yard, or teach them how to start their own garden.

Another powerful way to build community is to join several neighbors together and form a community garden. You may have noticed an empty lot near your home that could use some love. Empty lots invite crime, from inappropriate graffiti to more serious trespasses. Garden spaces, however, improve local property values,[81] reduce crime, and provide a place for children to learn and play safely. Gardens and green spaces help cool asphalt-overheated cities, reducing energy costs and giving residents a break from summer heat waves. Growing a garden as a group can help reduce the costs of water and other resources, like tools and compost. A community garden feeds the people and the land.

You may already have a garden in your community, but you may need to start one yourself. To start your own, gather a group of interested neighbors, and identify the issues and opportunities your community faces in forming a garden. Your first challenge may be to find a space. Or it might be to identify what an already available space offers in terms of constraints or opportunities. To reclaim an empty lot, contact local officials to see who owns the lot and what was on it previously. Find out about any area restrictions for development—not to stop you from creating a community garden, but to understand what regulations you will need to overcome in the process.

As a group, develop a shared vision. What would you and your group like to see happen with your lot or within your community? Maybe you need a safe play space, a garden that is wheelchair accessible, a place to grow the organic vegetables not offered by your local supermarket, or a local space for artwork. Perhaps you want to create jobs for local teens, or donate extra food to food banks. Maybe you would like to also restore the creek behind the lot and turn it into a nature center for schools to visit.

Next, create a plan involving goals, actions, and deadlines that will bring your vision to fruition. Make sure your entire group is involved in the plan and in taking action. Set a timeline and stick to it. Enlist outside help if necessary.

Identify within your group and its network what resources you possess. Find out who has gardening experience, fundraising skills, artistic ability, and so on. Who might be your potential partners and allies? Consider local schools, businesses, neighborhood associations, city council representatives, churches, and other residents. Include in your plan the development of these resources and strengths.

Then celebrate your accomplishments and milestones. In a world that tends to wait in fear for action to happen, you and your community have worked together to create a powerful force for positive change. Even small accomplishments can reap great rewards.[82]

You can also use the above guidelines in starting other garden projects, like a farmers' market, gardening cooperative, or grassroots school garden. What would you like to see bloom in your community?

If a community garden space already exists near your home, get involved and ask how you can help best serve the community to develop it into an even greater resource for neighbors. Offer classes on organic gardening, communicating with allies, or native flora and fauna. If you don't have a local Community Supported Agriculture program, consider working with your local community garden to set one up. By working with others, identify how garden spaces can offer resources for support and transformation. Gardening on the community level could begin a metamorphosis of city living. As Toby Hemenway, author of *Gaia's Garden,* writes, "Our yards, city parks, curbsides, even parking lots and office courtyards could be lush, productive, and attractive landscapes that aid nature while yielding much for us as well, instead of being the grassy emptinesses that they are."[83] By planting one garden at a time and linking communities together, we can grow a culture of interdependence from the ground up.

Sacred Sister: Judy Elliott

director of education and community empowerment, denver urban gardens

Called "Jungle Judy" by her students at one of Denver's inner-city schools, this gardening sacred sister teaches youth about perseverance and adaptability. When Denver's fickle weather or vandals destroy the students' organic garden, instead of giving up or responding with further violence, these youth learn about how they can be the proponents of change. Her students come up with solutions as they learn "new ways of seeing differences as a strength." Working together, these students with few resources learn about the power of diversity. They see how their own strengths can contribute to the community, and how nurturing others—both people and plants—makes them stronger.

In addition to gardening with teens, Judy also works with children with emotional and mental disabilities. These children learn about self-acceptance in the challenges and joys of the garden. They develop greater sensory awareness and motor skills. They find hope and a reflection of the natural flow of life by working together with each other and the land.

Judy told me the story of one girl suffering from a variety of challenges, including developmental delay, obsessive-compulsive disorder, and paranoia. After three years of spending time in the garden and being gently encouraged, this girl could finally place her hand on the soil. With further gentle support, she was able to place weeds on the shovel and carry them to the compost; eventually she was able to chop up the weeds and help mix them in to the pile. Not only did she learn about perseverance and courage, she was able to become an active member of her community.

Judy and her colleagues at DUG also offer the Denver area support in setting up organic community gardens. They teach people about the value of gardens, including the power of creating together in a diverse community and then sitting down to eat together at the same table. DUG and other organizations like them have shown how urban gardens increase property values and reduce crime. Through investment in a local garden space, community members become neighborhood activists and leaders. They learn that "the same thing we need for high-level living in plants we need in people," and they learn to apply those lessons to their own lives. The children and adults served by DUG discover a way of life that increases assets through community instead of focusing on lack or fear.[84]

Air Resources

Community Gardens

American Community Gardening Association
℅ Franklin Park Conservatory
1777 East Broad Street
Columbus, OH 43203
(877) ASK-ACGA or
(877) 275-2242
www.communitygarden.org

Offers training and networking for community garden spaces.

City Farmer
Vancouver, BC
Canada
(604)685-5832
www.cityfarmer.org

Their website has endless resources in the form of articles, images, and video clips.

Community Greens
1700 N. Moore Street, Suite 2000
Arlington, VA 22209-1939
(703) 527-8300
www.communitygreens.org

Not only a great resource to help you get started, their site also includes stories of community parks around the United States.

Denver Urban Gardens
3377 Blake Street, Suite 113
Denver, CO 80205
(303) 292-9900
www.dug.org

Celebrating twenty years of community gardens in 2005, DUG is one of several city-based organic gardening networks. They publish a quarterly newsletter full of stories and ideas, *The Underground News*.

Oakland Butterfly and Urban Gardens
1724 Mandela Parkway #5
Oakland, CA 94607
(510) 465-4660
www.obugs.org

Another resource for getting started; their website also includes stories of neighborhood gardens. You may have a local organization like DUG or OBUGS; contact the American Community Garden Association (listed above) for information.

Seattle Tilth Association
4649 Sunnyside Avenue North, #1
Seattle, WA 98103-6900
(206) 633-0451
tilth@seattletilth.org
www.seattletilth.org

Founded in 1978, Seattle Tilth is a nationally recognized nonprofit organization dedicated to cultivating a sustainable community, one garden at a time. In their demonstration gardens and community gardens across the region, they teach people how to improve their environment by using organic gardening techniques.

There are hundreds of community garden associations in the U.S., and those listed above are but a few. Contact ACGA for local information.

Center for Democracy and Citizenship
Humphrey Institute of Public Affairs
301 19th Avenue South
Minneapolis, MN 55455
(612) 625-0142
www.publicwork.org

Dedicated to taking democracy back into the hands of the people; a great resource for community organizing and research on working together from the ground up.

Conservation

For information on reducing pesticide use and taking action worldwide to protect our air allies through the banning of pesticides, contact the Pesticide Action Network of North America (PANNA).

Pesticide Action Network North America
49 Powell St., Suite 500
San Francisco, CA 94102
(415) 981-1771
(415) 981-1991
www.panna.org

Bat Conservation International
P.O. Box 162603
Austin, TX 78716
(512) 327-9721
www.batcon.org

Offers information on bats and bat conservation.

For more information on bees, see:

The International Bee Research Association
18 North Road,
Cardiff, CF10 3DT, UK
+44 (0) 29 2037 2409
www.ibra.org.uk/

Notes

NOTES

CHAPTER 3

Fire

it's a righteous fire
that makes you
shake your behind
makes you sit up straight
sign your name on the line
costs you nothing you'll miss
to inhabit your mind
it's a righteous fire …

Tony Edelblute,
"No Name Thing"

GODDESS

Amaterasu

Japanese ruling clans traced their heritage from the great sun goddess Omikami Amaterasu. "Heavenly Shining Great Female Person" protects the Japanese people, and her image of the rising sun is still featured on the Japanese flag.

Call on Amaterasu to bless your garden and assure a balanced amount of heat and light. Thank her when eating the crisp and nourishing vegetables that depended on her to grow. If you struggle with your own inner fire, she can help you come out of your cave; she will reflect to you your beauty and potential.

The Sun

Everything on Earth comes from the sun, and like souls reaching for the Goddess, all things seek the light and energy of this nearest star. Plants reach out for its power, animals munch on the plants who have transformed the light, while stones bask and water evaporates into the shining sky. The sun fuels our passions and the change we enact in the world. Step into your garden to witness a hallelujah chorus of reverence for the sun as green beings constantly transform light energy into food.

The sun is a ball of hydrogen and helium interacting under intense pressure; when these elements collide, the resulting transformation releases energy. Containing 99.8 percent of the total mass of the solar system, the sun holds us in a firm gravitational embrace. It is 1.39 million kilometers in diameter. At its core, Sol burns at 15.6 million Kelvin, while the surface of the star is much cooler, only 5800 Kelvin (9,980° Fahrenheit). It's about 4.5 billion years old, a middle-aged star.[85] It is certainly no wonder that ancient peoples worshiped the sun as a deity.

Among the aboriginal peoples of Australia, the sun is a goddess who wakes each day in her camp in the east, lights her fire, and prepares the torch she will carry across the sky. She paints herself with red ochre, some of which spills and turns the clouds red. At the end of the day she reapplies her paint, spilling some into the red clouds of sunset. At night she travels beneath the earth, warming the land from beneath so the plants can grow.

Malina is the sun goddess of the Inuit peoples of Greenland. She too travels across the sky carrying a torch, but she is chased by her brother, the moon. In Norse mythology, the goddess Sol is also pursued—by a wolf named Skoll. Sol rides a chariot pulled by the horses Alsvid and Arvak, who have manes of fire. To the Incas, the sun was called Inti, and he was married to Pachamama, the earth goddess. Their children taught humans about civilization. The Fon people of West Africa saw the sun as a creation god named Liza, who formed Earth using his son Gu in the shape of a great sword. Liza is also the god of heat, work, and strength.[86]

In some traditional sun myths, the deity has little to do with humans, while in others he or she regularly interacts with us. Scientifically speaking, both are true: Earth receives only about two billionths of the sun's energy, a relatively small parcel of quanta that creates a green and growing Earth housing billions of people, plants, animals, insects, and other beings. The sun's gift of energy makes earthly life possible.

The garden is a place to marvel at the power of fire to ignite life. Scientists believe that life came about when lightning struck water, forming the first amino acids. The building blocks of proteins, RNA, and DNA, amino acids help us synthesize the molecules we use to think, grow, and take in sensory information. We cannot manufacture most of the twenty amino acids used to build protein on our own, so we take them in through food; free amino acids, those not already combined into proteins and therefore easier to utilize, are available in the plants we grow in the garden. Plants create these key molecules, as well as sugars and starch, by basking in the sun.

Physicist Dr. Larry Edwards argues that photosynthesis is the greatest technology ever created on Earth.[87] The beings who created the ability to transform light into food set the stage for most of the living processes on earth. Photosynthesis enables us to utilize the sun's fire as fuel, transforming it into the energy we use on Earth, from the food we eat to the fossil fuels we burn. Fire, then, is about energy, transformation, and power.

Plants gather and use the power of transformation, passing it onto us through the magic of a cup of tea, the passion of orchids, the antioxidants in a tomato. They store it in their seeds, sending it to the next generation of green beings. You can find plant fire in the tenacity and potency of herbs, wild plants, and heirloom varieties. We sisters can reflect plant fire by living passionately through ritual, activism, and personal transformation. In this chapter we will explore all of the aspects of fire in the garden.

Seeds

Like the Little Engine That Could, tiny seeds pack a lot of power: they are the sparks of life created by a plant's interaction with the sun. Whether large as the twenty kilogram double coconut seed or tiny as a celery seed, seeds are high in nutrients like protein and fat, for they provide the energy necessary to get a baby plant started. This baby plant will grow many times the size of its seeds, producing tens or hundreds or even thousands more seeds in its lifecycle. A seed carries life and makes life possible.

Kathleen Harrison, an associate of the nonprofit Seeds of Change, said, "Each seed is encoded with the DNA story. Each seed is a long, winding, subtle story. The seeds have crossed human hands and been cultivated by us, and selected by us and bred out, and traded across continents and oceans now, and saved from extinction at the last minute, and lost forever as well. These are all really the voices of the ancestors speaking in each of those seeds."[88]

South American indigenous peoples hold that seeds carry the wisdom and wealth of the land and their ancestors. Quechua Indians keep corn seeds in their pockets, mixed with money, for corn represents life, fortune, and happiness. Seeds are power, for who has seeds has food and life.

A seed is actually a fertilized ovule. Many seeds contain a plant embryo surrounded by the endosperm, or food storage tissue; the thickness of the endosperm depends on the type of plant. The whole package of embryo and food is then surrounded by a seed coat, or testa. Some "seeds" are actually fruits, which are mature, ripened ovaries containing seeds. The endosperm, testa, and fruit coat are mostly made of "maternal tissue," or matter from the female part of the plant. Seeds are tiny goddesses sparked by the god to create life.

Some seeds are viable for thousands of years, going dormant until the right conditions exist for germination. For a seed to germinate, it may need to be soaked, frozen, burned, or consumed by an animal. When the conditions are right, the embryo bursts the seed coat by soaking up water and sends out the first tiny root. When I germinate seeds in wet paper towels, the nutrient-seeking root reminds me of my baby daughter "rooting" for the breast. Their little "mouths" purposefully squirm about in search of food. Shortly after the rootling pops out, the plant matter that will form the stem and leaves unfolds in search of light. Then these tiny plants can grow through brick, if necessary, to find the energy they seek.

A seed's desire to grow literally makes a garden possible, but it also represents the magic of the garden. When you plant seeds, approach them with the love and respect you would an infant human. Place them in the earth gently, with mindfulness. This intention will live in the seed and grow as a part of the fabric of your plants. When the plant dies, it will return gratitude and respect back into the earth.

Garden seeds do best in loose soil rich with organic matter. They need to be moist to germinate and close enough to the soil surface to reach light quickly. The soil surrounding the seeds must be evenly moist but not soggy, and fairly warm. You may wish to start seeds indoors or in a greenhouse in sterile planting soil, but you can also begin your seeds right in the garden. The technique I prefer is to germinate the seeds first, then plant them carefully in prepared soil containing lots of compost, well-composted manure, and peat moss or vermiculite. To germinate seeds, place them between two sheets of damp paper towels and place in a plastic bag or container. Set in a warm place like the top of the refrigerator or hot water heater. Check them daily, spritzing the paper towel to keep it moist. As soon as little roots have emerged, plant the germinated seed in a pot or directly in the garden. If the weather is still cool (especially night temperatures) or you have a problem with nosy squirrels, cover the baby seeds with a mini greenhouse or hoop tunnel made from plastic sheeting stretched over a metal or wooden frame. A gallon milk jug with the bottom cut off also makes a simple mini greenhouse. Keep the cap on when the weather is cool, and remove to vent your little greenhouse during the heat of the day.

Keep the little seeds moist; while they have already germinated, they are still very vulnerable. As they grow, you may need to keep them covered at night, or provide shade at the hottest point of the afternoon by covering them with shade cloth or a screen.

Some plants do better seeded directly into the soil,

like corn and beans, while others do best transplanted into the garden bed when they are already established. Tomatoes, peppers, and eggplant are among those that need more controlled conditions to germinate, and they do best planted in flats or small pots in a protected space like a greenhouse, coldframe, or sunny window. Which plants you choose to grow will depend on your climate, if you have space for a nursery (or wish to buy transplants from a local nursery), and the growing needs for each plant.

Whether germinated or ungerminated, plant seeds as deep as its vertical dimension. Traditionally, seeds are planted in rows, spaced closer along the row than between each row. Long rows go the length of a bed or field, while short rows are planted across a bed's width and are useful for smaller gardens. The French Intensive Method plants seeds in a honeycomb pattern, spacing them not in rows but hexagonally spaced clumps, with each seed the same distance from all the seeds around it. Mel Bartholomew, inventor of the Square Foot Gardening Method, plants a grid of squares, putting only as many plants as will fit in a square foot; a spot will fit one cabbage, sixteen carrots, or four heads of leaf lettuce, equally spaced in a square foot. You could even plant in circles or spirals. There is no right way to arrange seeds, as long as they have enough room to grow and you can reach them with ease at harvest time.

We will revisit seeds at the end of this chapter, when we explore the art of seed saving.

Fire Ally: Salamander

The amphibeous salamander divides her life between water and land. *Amphi-* means "double" and *bio-* means "life." Salamander energy is therefore about the double lives we all lead to some degree and the transitions we must face as we move through our different selves. They can teach us about the dream world, the world of water and emotion. Since salamanders hear low tones, to gain greater sensitivity to the realms of the Underworld, drum or play the didgeridoo to enter a trancelike meditative state.

It was once believed that salamanders were made of fire. They make their homes in rotted logs, and when those logs were tossed on a fire, the frightened beings scurried out of the flames. People believed the animals were borne of fire. The fire-born mythological salamander is therefore the elemental of fire, the consciousness of flame. She weaves brightly colored, fireproof garments that mimic the camouflage designs on her back, so if you face a challenging life situation, call on Salamander to clothe you in protection. Call on her to safely burn away the past as you transform into a new being and as you do your work as a sacred sister, transforming the world through your own inner fire.

Enhancing Fire Energy in the Garden

When you go through times of transformation or wish to cultivate change in the world, it can be helpful to have a place to meditate on fire energy. Bring more fire into the garden to honor the powers of rebirth burning in your life or to enhance passionate times, like parties and outdoor lovemaking. Tiki torches and safe candle receptacles literally boost the fire energy in a yard, but you can also include plants and stones in your garden design whose energy is of fire.

Fire stones and metals include:

- Agate, amber, apache tear, bloodstone, brass, orange calcite, carnelian, citrine, diamond, flint, garnet, gold, hematite, iron, red jasper, mica, obsidian, onyx, pyrite, quartz crystal, ruby, steel, sunstone, tiger's-eye, topaz, red tourmaline, and zircon.[89]

To include fire minerals in your garden, create a walkway, patio, or birdbath studded with these stones. Include brass or gold-colored ornaments, or paint your fence ruby or gold. If you seek more fire energy in your life, build a fire altar in the garden, perhaps in the south. Surround your altar with any of the following fire plants:

- Alder, anemone, angelica, ash, basil, bay, betony, black snakeroot, blood root, cactus, carnation, carrot, cat tail, cedar, celery, chestnut, chrysanthemum, cinquefoil, coriander (cilantro seed), dill, fennel, fig, flax, garlic, ginseng, goldenseal, gorse, hawthorn, heliotrope, holly, hyssop, juniper, leek, lovage, marigold, mullein, mustard, oak, olive, onion, pine, pennyroyal, peppermint, radish, rosemary, rue, St. John's wort, shallot, snapdragon, sunflower, thistle, woodruff, and yucca.[90]

Fire Ally: Snake

Snake is a fire ally who can guide us along the winding path of transformation.

A relative of dragon, snake carries the fire of kundalini, the awakening of enlightenment coiled at the base of the spine. In many cultures, snake represents rebirth and eternal life, for she sheds her skin to emerge a new being several times in her life. Snakes also represent knowledge and passion.

One of the original stories of Eve says that initially in the garden she lived alone with her serpent, a creature she created for her sexual pleasure.[91] The goddess Chantico wears a red snake about her neck as a sign of passion and power. In India, the serpent goddess Kadru is said to have birthed the immortal cobra people, feeding them with her lunar blood. The church stifled this feminine sexual power by associating the serpent with the devil and fire with eternal damnation and pain. The church fathers feared the bite of transformation and death and saw sexuality and women, we who can birth new life like a snake sheds her skin, as evil.

Today this is changing, however slowly, and women are reconnecting with the energy of Kali, goddess of both creation and destruction. Humanity is slowly healing our fearful relationship with death. Snake, as one of the teachers on this journey, reminds us that though life may change the way it looks, truly it is a coiled spiral of rebirth. As snake sheds her skin, there comes a time when we must shed this life when we grow too large for our bodies, either physically or spiritually or both. Snake guards the hidden knowledge of the afterlife and the Underworld. She moves silently but quickly and brings swift change, awakening creativity and personal power.

Snakes in the garden fill an important ecological niche, keeping rodent and insect populations in balance. We generally think of snakes as being solitary creatures, but many species gather for mating, basking, and birthing their young. Female snakes, especially sisters, congregate during pregnancy and in the first weeks after giving birth to protect their young and each other from predators. They form social groups with "extensive contact among related individuals across generations," writes herpetologist Rulon Clark, who studies the timber rattlesnake. There is evidence that snakes organize in matrilineal groups,[92] little covens of transformation and rebirth.

Depending on where you live, you may share space with harmless garter snakes or with rattlers and other poisonous biters. A snake that rattles or rears up is merely trying to look scary. She herself is scared or is defending her nest. A good response to a frightened snake is simply to back away or stand very still and let it slither away. Thank her for keeping the local rodent populations down, let your entire body be calm, and let her escape. Then, when you are safely away from the startled snake, meditate on snake energy in your life. What transformation do you face? What healing path do you follow? How strong is your own life force? Begin to examine how Snake enters your life and what she may have to teach you about the spiral of life.

GODDESS

Chantico

Aztec goddess of fire, home, and fertility, Chantico teaches us that pain and pleasure can occur simultaneously in the center of passion, love, and the labor of birth. She teaches us about living the dialectic that life insists. She is a cactus, sharp but abundant with water.

While all of the elements hold the powers of creation and destruction, we tend to see this reality most immediately in fire, the life-giving heat that can lick away everything we hold dear in an instant.

To help understand your relationship with this dynamic element, call on Chantico. Her symbol is the red snake, and she brings us wealth and protection.[93] In the garden, honor her with a spiky cactus planted in red stone, or grow fiery peppers or paprika, perhaps in a red pot studded with gems.

Herbs

Perhaps the most concentrated energy of transformation and healing in the garden is found in herbs. Used for medicinal, culinary, or magical purposes, herbs can easily be incorporated into any stewardship garden.

When I was fifteen, I planted my first garden. I had grown up helping my father in his vegetable garden, but the first plot of my own, dug on the side of the house by my bedroom window, I planted with herbs. I am not sure what initially attracted me to herbs, except maybe a fantasy about a wise old woman living in a cottage by the sea, tending her herbs and healing the villagers. At fifteen I was a far cry from this alter ego, but something about the magic of herbs attracted me. In that first plot I grew sage, lavender, mints, lemon balm, and other common favorites. For Christmas my mother gave me a book on herbs, and I learned about the history of my friends as well as how to use them for beauty, household decorating, and cooking. In college I had the opportunity to gather wild herbs in the sun of southern France with a lovely Provençal woman named Cécile. She showed me and a friend where to gather rosemary and thyme from the dry fields near her 400-year-old farmhouse. I felt connected to the great fire-soaked wisdom of these wild herbs and all the women before me who had walked these paths formed before the Romans came to France.

Years later I learned about the magical qualities of herbs, but I initially related to this information as being quaint and fantastical. I saw it as mere superstition that wearing a posy of violets and marjoram during the winter would protect one from getting a cold, or that eating coriander while pregnant would make one's unborn child a genius.

I discovered, however, the immense power in herbs when I learned to connect with the energy of a plant directly. I feel psychic information kinesthetically, so when I attune with a plant I get a felt sense of its personality, gifts, and propensities. I find that each plant has its own signature, and that while some plants are sweet and gentle, others can knock me off my feet with their intensity. Many herbs hold this quality for me, and I wonder now if my draw to herbs as a teenager came from this immense power; I sensed it then but was not yet attuned enough to my extended senses to name what I felt.

In feeling into herbs' powers, I discovered that their magical qualities were not mere superstition. Everything in the universe is a vibration, and that vibration radiates out beyond an object's physical boundaries. All of the vibrations of everything around you create a matrix in which you live, create, and grow. Just as a sound vibration will cause things around it to vibrate at its frequency, vibrations of various objects affect the other objects and beings in their fields. Those fields can be immediate, like the room you are in right now, or infinite, including everything in the universe. Wearing, eating, or even connecting at a distance to an herb (or anything else, for that matter) will bring you into attunement with that herb's frequency. Making magic with herbs—from cups of tea to love potions—involves attuning to its vibration, which shifts your own vibration toward your intended goal.

Herbs are very powerful, fiery little creatures. Little vortexes of particular energies, they help to intensify these energies in us and their environment. While herbal guides are helpful to learn more about a plant's properties, far more important for powerful magic-making is to personally connect with the plant itself and learn from that listening. Study herbals if you are drawn to work with them, but do not let others' words substitute for your own direct experience of and relationship with herbs. True magic, be it manifestation, healing, or learning, comes from within you and your relationship with the world, not from rules or lists. To work with herbs, cultivate relationships with them. As with all sacred gardening, making magic with herbs is collaborative and co-creative.

Herbs can be incorporated into the garden in several ways. You may wish to devote a specific section of land to a healing garden just for herbs, or plant a kitchen garden with cooking herbs near the kitchen door. Herbs enjoy being planted throughout the garden, as well, through companion planting. Group them with other plants that use similar amounts of water or could benefit from their gifts. Plant the following herbs anywhere in the garden to attract beneficial insects or repel pests:

- Basil, bee balm, caraway, chives, coriander, daisy, dill, garlic, hyssop, lavender, lemon balm, lovage, marigold, marjoram, mint, parsley, pennyroyal, tansy, thyme, wormwood, and yarrow.

To avoid the more aggressive plants like yarrow and mint from taking over your entire garden, plant them in containers. Ask the land what herbs would be a good fit for your purposes, like healing or to raise energies on the land.

One way to work with herbs is to make a tea, incense, salve, smoking mixture, smudge stick, or some other herbal preparation. Herbs can be used fresh, in tinctures, on salads, or dried in teas and infusions. You can make your own salves quite easily by gently heating your herb of choice in olive or almond oil over low heat for about fifteen minutes, straining the infused oil, and mixing in beeswax until melted. Pour into little containers and cool. To learn more about making magical herbal concoctions, see Fire Resources for suggested herbals.

It is not just the use of the herb, like drinking or burning, that taps into the herb's power, but the whole process of gathering, preparing, using, and relating to the herb that attunes us to its energy and gifts. For that reason, you do not need to create any sort of potion or tea to attune with an herb; you can simply sit with it and listen.

If you have never worked directly with herbal energies, you might begin your practice with rosemary, a common but powerful herb. Take a few breaths and connect with the earth. Center your body by paying attention for a few moments to the sensations you encounter right now. Hold in front of you a rosemary plant (or any other herb you have available). You can use cut herbs from a local farmers' market, a growing plant, or even simply draw to your attention the energy of the herb. Say hello to the plant, and ask it for permission to connect with its energy. If you get an affirmative response, go deeper into sensing, using your mind's eye/ear/felt sense to connect with and sense the plant's energetic frequency. Notice the personality of the plant. What do you sense? What do you learn about the plant's gifts? Pay special attention to what happens in your body—does your heart rate change? Does your mood change? Before reading any further, spend time with this plant and write down what you sense or discover in your garden journal. Do not worry about either being correct or imaginative and making things up.

Now that you have your own experience of rosemary, let us look at what herbalists and magicians have to say about the herb. Cunningham, in his *Encyclopedia of Magical Herbs,* writes that rosemary is masculine and allied with the sun and fire. Its powers include protection, love, lust, mental powers, exorcism, purification, healing, sleep, and youth. It rids negativity, ensures good sleep, purifies the body, and promotes healing.[94] David Hoffman, in *The New Holistic Herbal,* tells us that *Rosmarinus officinalis* is a circulatory and nervine stimulant.[95] It promotes digestion and reduces depression by reducing physiological stress. It is also anti-parasitic and antiseptic.[96] How does this magical and medicinal information compare with what you discovered in your chat with rosemary?

Since herbs are such strong beings with very specific energies, they love to help us in our transformational work such as healing and personal growth. This is an aspect of their fire energy. Part of their reason for being on the planet is to contribute to the consciousness of the whole Earth. Working either medicinally or magically with herbs taps into this powerful gift.

Herbs can be used medicinally or magically, though the most powerful work with these green allies incorporates and integrates all aspects of the plants. Challenge yourself to look at all aspects of an issue: the physical, emotional, and spiritual dimensions. Nothing is just physical or just emotional; for instance, the flu often involves some sort of resistance or fear, while a love affair affects your sleep and heart rate as well as your emotional self. Herbs are equally multifaceted and love to contribute to all the energies of an issue. Take a common life challenge, that of cultivating a healthy relationship with money and finances. Many magical responses to this issue tend to involve burning herbal incense said to increase luck and money while praying or meditating. Yet consider how finances affect you physically: how does it feel in your body when you are broke or when you receive a windfall? Where could you use some support, and how might herbs help with this?

This multifaceted approach requires a certain honesty with oneself in addition to a relationship with herbal energies. With a money issue, for instance, it requires that you admit to your fears about following a budget, not just your desire for lots of money. Rarely does more money solve a person's financial problems. Until these hidden issues like fear, self-worth, and resistance are addressed, financial problems will not just go away—and certainly not from simply burning a special blend of incense and chanting in rhyme.

Herbs actually find this abracadabra approach to magic insulting. Remember, magic happens when we encounter the divine. Herbs are like any tools or beings in that they help you to align with divine energy, and it is that relationship that results in "magic."

Susun Weed refers to herbs as green allies, which captures the role they can play in our lives. An ally is not just a friend but one who supports us against attack. Sometimes this means calling us on our flaws and fears, which at times doesn't feel very friendly. It can feel quite uncomfortable to look at one's own challenges or fears, and while herbs try to be gentle allies, they deserve our respect as the wise and intense beings they are.

When working with herbs, therefore, always do so with respect. Give them thanks, ask for their input, and treat them with the reverence they deserve. Your herbal creations will be stronger for it, and your change and growth will be more meaningful.

GODDESS

Airmid

Airmid, Herbwife,
Mistress of the healing green, We call on Thee:
Turn our gardens with the Nourishing Earth,
Twine our forests with the Sight Beyond Sight...
Here we have planted holy herbs
Pleasing to Thee, shaped in the long snakes
Of sacred knotwork. Come walk among them
And be welcome now.
—from *Greenwitch* by Elizabeth Barrette[97]

HEAR AIRMID WHISPER her wisdom of the wise women's secrets of green ways. The Celtic goddess of herbs and herb lore, Airmid guides you gently into the powerful world of her allies. Trust the power of her strong hands, which will hold your body and soul in her loving grasp until you are once again whole.

To honor Airmid in your garden, carve a rough-hewn face in a log. Place before her visage a silver or stone bowl of water or simply a patch of your favorite herb. Spend time in your garden, soaking up the healing power of the green, and give thanks to the Celtic mother Airmid.

Call on her as you mix herbal potions and teas and as you add healing herbs to your food. She will bless the alchemy of your potion.

Sacred Sister: Rosemary Gladstar

herbalist

I have learned much about plants and being a woman of power from sacred sister Rosemary Gladstar. One of the country's best loved and most well-known herbalists, Gladstar is co-founder of the Sage Mountain Herbal Retreat Center and Botanical Sanctuary in central Vermont. She is the president of the United Plant Savers, an organization dedicated to protecting and renewing threatened medicinal plants. She has written *Herbal Healing for Women* and *Rosemary Gladstar's Family Herbal* and edited *Planting the Future: Saving Our Medicinal Herbs.* She is a plant warrior dedicated to bringing peace through the power of plants, saving medicinal and endangered plants from extinction, and teaching others about sacred living on the earth.

Rosemary first became interested in plants as a girl growing up on a farm in Sonoma County. Her grandmother, a strong Armenian woman, taught Rosemary about the wisdom of wild plants, as did the plants themselves. In one of her earliest dreams, she met the spirit of Oak and learned to listen to the plants through dreams as well as working directly with them. She teaches that the best way to learn about herbs is to work with them directly, to know them first before you turn to books or teachers to tell you about their properties. For her, this doesn't only mean talking with the plant spirits, which can be intimidating for some people, but simply noticing and honoring what you see, smell, or feel.

She does feel that at this time the plants are calling to us, asking for our help to protect and restore them. She says that this is "the honor of living on this planet right now," the ability to make a difference.

She writes,

> With the recent events in the world, it brings to heart ever more deeply how important it is that we hold the light in our beings and learn what we must about living lightly upon this earth. The plants are among our best teachers. And reminding people how to be in relationship with plants, how to enter into their green world to receive their sacred teachings, is as powerful a "medicine" as one can learn/teach at this time on earth.[98]

To be in relationship with plants, she teaches, requires listening to all the ways they might communicate. Plants communicate with us "if we but choose to listen," and they are calling to us to help them. In *Planting the Future,* Rosemary offers some of the ways we can help save them:

Be a conscious and responsible consumer: Know the herb products you use and the herb companies you purchase from. Only buy sustainably harvested herbs.

Grow your own medicines: Grow organically herbs you use frequently for cooking or healing; include local native plants and at-risk wild plants. For information on at-risk plants, see *Planting the Future* (see Fire Resources, "Herbs").

Restore wilderness areas on your land: Devote an area to native plants and noninvasive weeds. Provide sanctuary for lizards, butterflies, and other wildlife. Invite the devas to run the land.

Go native: Plant a native medicinal plant trail or even a native plot in your garden. To find out what grows native in your area, contact local herb schools, United Plant Savers (see Fire Resources), or your local extension office. Learn how to use these plants through sustainable harvest. Invite neighbors to explore and learn from your trail or garden.

Eat herbs: Cultivate and consume weedy herbs for general wellness to reduce use of at-risk herbs intended for specific healing purposes. For example, eat plenty of burdock and dandelion to support liver functioning and a healthy immune system, reducing your need for emergency immune builders like osha and echinacea, which have been commercially overharvested.

Be mindful of groups on wildcrafting expeditions: Be gentle on the land, especially when there are a lot of you searching for wild herbs.[99]

Through her beautiful books and her bright presence, Rosemary teaches us that being a fiery, active woman in tune with the powers of the earth does not mean giving up gentleness or a calm center. She teaches the importance of listening to the earth and taking action to restore humanity's relationship with wilderness while remaining centered in the wisdom held in our own bones.

Planting a Wild Garden

It may seem like an oxymoron to cultivate wild plants, but providing sanctuary for wild beings in our own gardens is a powerful way to protect, preserve, and honor the passionate powers of wilderness. The sacred land includes not just food and flowers, but the wilderness as well.

To bring wild plants into your garden or create a wild area on your land, begin by talking with local wildflower societies and researching your local native plants. Go for walks in your neighborhood and local woods, and observe what grows there. Learn to identify local plants, as well as local invasive weeds. Identify the microclimates of your own land to identify what types of native and wild plants will thrive in your garden. Include fruits, berries, and seeds as well as plants and mini-habitats that provide shelter to support local wildlife.

Native plants can be incorporated into your food and flower gardens in what those who practice permaculture call *guilds*. A guild is a miniature ecosystem of plants and animals that is created by the gardener to benefit humans as well as animals and the plants themselves. It includes a collection of mutually beneficial plants that serve multiple purposes. A guild incorporating food plants and native plants might include a pear tree, a native berry bush, comfrey for nutrients and leaf mulch, clover for ground cover and nitrogen, and a noninvasive native grass to prevent erosion. For more on guilds and permaculture, a vast and important branch of ecologically sustainable gardening, see Toby Hemenway's *Gaia's Garden: A Guide to Home-Scale Permaculture.*

Native gardens and ecological guild-focused gardens provide valuable opportunities to teach others about the land. Open your native garden to others, through yearly garden tours, classes given on your land, or simply an invitation to neighborhood children and adults. Find others in your area with whom to learn and collaborate on projects that further develop wilderness areas in your city or town. Invite children, elders, and people outside your regular circles to join you.

Observe how the native energies of your land affect you, your family, and your community. What does wilderness bring into your life? What do native plant energies teach you about the place you have chosen as your home? If you find yourself living in a place you did not consciously choose, what can you learn about adapting to present circumstances through the teachings of these plants?

Fire is about transformation. What does it mean to transform our cultivated and safe lands back into their wild selves? What does it mean to invite the power of nature into your own life? What can it teach you about taking action and responsibility for your world? Plants that are native to your area improve soil quality, require less water, and are generally hardy against local pests. They support the local wildlife, perhaps 10 to 50 times more than imported species. How can you see this affecting your own energy, from your immune system to your sense of home to your relationships with others?

With permission from the plants, you may want to hold rituals of passion in your wild garden. The energies of nature may be especially strong in your wild garden, so magic working and meditation can be a wild ride in a wilderness setting. A space where you have consciously invited in devic energy can offer a delightful circle of energy in which to play.

GODDESS

Goga

THE GODDESS OF fire and sacred ceremony, Goga renews her strength and immortality with a magical fire within. She taught the people of New Guinea how to work, play, and do ritual with fire. At first she kept her primal fire a secret, but a boy stole a brand of fire from her; as he ran from her wrath, he accidentally lit a tree on fire. Though Goga tried to stifle the fire with a great deluge, a large snake preserved the flame on his tail, and the first humans used this smoldering flame to light the first fire.[100]

Call on Goga as your own fire awakens and as you do rituals of transformation in the garden.

The Wheel of the Year

A living altar, the garden is a place to honor the change of the seasons and the great bounty gifted by the earth. The Celtic or pagan celebrations of the cycling of seasons are known as the sabbats, which celebrate the eight solar changes: the equinoxes, solstices, and the four holidays at cross quarters to these seasonal markers. Together these holy days make up the Wheel of the Year, the celebration of life and the sun.

Celebrating these seasonal markers comes naturally in the garden, for the sabbats are simply days to formally recognize the shifting light, changing temperatures, and seasons of growing. You may honor them with a full-blown festival or a simple, private recognition. Many of our Western secular holidays actually get much of their traditions from the sabbats, like the Yule tree, Maypole, and Thanksgiving cornucopia, so it can actually be quite easy to incorporate your celebrations into holidays you are used to. The sabbats are less about one specific day and more about time set aside to give thanks for the gifts of the Earth, whether that be the sparkle of snow or an overflowing basket of ripe tomatoes.

The Sabbats

Samhain: October 31 in Northern Hemisphere, May 1 in Southern Hemisphere.

Samhain, pronounced sow-in, is more commonly known as Halloween in the United States. Gardens this time of the year are droopy and spooky, rustling with the dried stalks of corn. Pumpkin vines have withered or dried, and the great orange or white orbs rise to their full power. Pick some for baking, choose a few to carve, and leave the rest to decorate the landscape. Do the same for any other gourds; wait until November to bring your squash into the root cellar if you can. Where I live, we often get our first snow right about Samhain, but it's usually just a dusting, so my gourds are safe outside.

One of my favorite smells comes from autumnal apples settling in for winter at the bases of their trees. Some might call it rotting. Gather the last apples from the tree and those from the ground that aren't too bruised for jam, cider, and sauce. Use a few mushy ones for target practice as you toss them into the compost bin. Remember to give thanks to the tree for its bounteous gift.

Buy a few straw bales from local farmers or Halloween fairs. Organic is best, for when the holiday has passed, you will mulch your garden beds with the straw. Set up a few bales in front of your door and around the yard. Decorate inside and out with dried flowers and seed heads from your landscape to honor this time of the final harvest. Don't throw those seed pods in the regular compost unless you like a lot of weedy volunteers (instead, use them to make compost tea).

To honor your ancestors and friends who have crossed over, go out into your garden after dark and set up a simple altar. Include a candle in a sturdy jar and a little wine or rum, and take a moment to give thanks for the gifts these spirits have given you. Sprinkle some of your liquid spirits on the earth as an offering. Send up a prayer of blessing to those who have walked before, and if you like, ask them for guidance. Take a moment to listen, and you will hear them in the wind through the browned leaves or smell them in the shift of seasons. They may also come to you in dreams, especially at this time of year when the veil between the worlds is quite thin.

Yule: December 21 in Northern Hemisphere, June 21 in Southern Hemisphere.

One of the most famous Yule celebrations is the *tannenbaum*, the evergreen brought indoors and decorated with trinkets and lights. Druids used to decorate oak trees at the time of the winter solstice, and the Egyptians decorated with palm leaves in honor of Isis. To Saint Boniface, the triangle-shaped evergreen represented the Christian Trinity and Christ's promise of eternal life. To pagans, the Yule tree represents the promise of the return of life even in the depths of winter, and some customs say we bring it indoors to give the wood sprites a warm place to stay through the dark time of the year. We decorate the tree with symbols of fertility, like fruits, nuts, and pine cones, and with images of light in honor of the birth of the Sun (or Son) King.

In my household, we often purchase a small live tree that we plant in spring, and we decorate our outdoor pines with seeds and ribbons for the birds. Most of our indoor ornaments represent something from nature, like walnuts, stars, and icicles.

I pay homage to the fairies with images of the great elf Santa, one of the only pagan gods worshiped by mainstream society. When choosing your tree, either live or cut, ask the devas and nature spirits for guidance and permission. Always give thanks for the gift.

In addition to your tree, decorate with boughs, berries, and homemade wreaths. One year I used the sucker shoots off our crabapple tree twined with ivy to make a lovely and simple wreath. Oranges and pomegranates are in season in warmer areas this time of year, so a few end up on my table and in stockings as well. A friend of mine brings in a plain branch fallen from a windstorm, sticks it into a bucket of sand, and decorates it with traditional ornaments. The branch's simple beauty is a testament to the season.

Light candles as a reminder of the return of light, the start of a new solar year. If you do not have time to make your own of beeswax and dried herbs, you can still anoint purchased candles with herb-soaked oils. Candles naturally scented with cedar, cinnamon, and clove bring alive the spirit of the season. A candle is literally a small piece of the sun, a reminder that all life and light come from our nearest star. What greater gift is there?

Give as gifts or serve at family meals any fruits or vegetables you preserved last fall, especially spiced plums and pears and brandied cherries. If you did not have the time to preserve, give thanks to those who made your store-bought preserved fruits. Consider what your greatest gift is to the world, and share that with your friends and family as your holiday gift: sing a song, write a poem, or bake a batch of world-famous cookies.

Imbolc: February 2 in Northern Hemisphere, August 2 in Southern Hemisphere.

Imbolc is Brigit's Day, known also as Candlemas and Oimelc. This marks the first flowing of the ewes' milk, a sign of spring on its way. Groundhog's Day and Valentine's Day both carry traditions of Imbolc, including marking the return of the light and love charms. The Bear Goddess emerges from her slumber to welcome her young ones into the light, and the crocus pokes through the snow to welcome her.

Imbolc is not as flashy a holiday as many others but is a time of quiet reverence and the beginning of the planting season. When you begin to smell spring on the wind, you may plant the first spring crops in coldframes or row covers. Plant peas, lettuce, arugula, and beets. If your land experiences warmer nights early, you might begin warmer season crops such as tomatoes in equally protected spots. Begin flats of broccoli and her cousins, and scatter annual and perennial seeds. Be sure to plant radishes—they do well in the cold and germinate quickly. I especially like the French radishes in the holiday colors of red and white. Many locations will get another dusting (or dumping!) of snow before spring, and the cool wetness will encourage growth.

Violets peek up this time of year, so gather their lovely flowers for syrup and tea. One of the miracles of violets is that the pretty purple flowers do not contain the reproductive organs of the plant; these come later as little yellow-green buds. So you can eat all the "flowers" you wish—they will grow many more flower heads and still seed prolifically. The violet has amazing yet gentle healing properties, especially for women. Violets gently heal the yoni, womb, and breasts. They can help reduce swelling, including tumors. Make a tincture by filling a jar with violet flowers and covering with vodka, then let it sit in a dark place for six weeks. Tinctures can be taken as twenty drops or more in a glass of water. For more immediate use, make an infusion, which is a strong tea, by covering a handful of violets with eight ounces of boiling water. Cover, let sit for ten minutes, and drink. They also make a nice cough syrup: cook a handful or two gently over low heat in a few cups of honey and a tablespoon of vinegar; cool and refrigerate. Consume within four to six weeks; the vinegar and honey act as preservatives, but moisture from the flowers can lead to spoilage. For more on making herbal solutions, see Rosemary Gladstar's *Family Herbal*.

You might also press them and decorate your Valentine's cards with violets and other spring flowers. Press them between a few pieces of paper in a heavy book to preserve, then glue them to cards. Or dry them, and use them in potpourri. Do not forget, though, to give thanks for your harvest by offering the gift of natural fertilizers, water, or blessing upon any flowers you gather.

Ostara: About March 21 in Northern Hemisphere,

September 21 in Southern Hemisphere.

The German goddess of spring gives her name to this sabbat, which eventually became Easter. The funny thing about Easter as a Christian holiday is that it falls after the first Sunday after the full moon following the vernal equinox, or Ostara. In other words, Easter's date is set by a "pagan" holy day. To avoid this heresy, the date of Easter is set not by the actual full moon, known as the astronomical full moon, but on the ecclesiastical full moon, the church-designated full moon that may or may not correspond with what happens in the sky. The old church feared following the actual orbits of the sun and moon, which would be far too pagan.

However, we who listen to the natural rhythms have been duped as well, for the actual equinox, which happens when the apparent longitude of the sun is zero degrees, shifts slightly from year to year. In other words, it does not always fall on March 21 (in the Northern Hemisphere), which is the date the church designated the ecclesiastical vernal equinox. The astronomical equinox may be different. To find out the actual occurrence of the equinox, check the National Weather Service or NOAA's websites or find a good nature-based calendar.

Regardless of when the day falls on the Gregorian calendar (the one hanging on your wall and programmed into your computer that was created by Pope Gregory XIII in 1582), this is a celebration of your hemisphere tilting back toward the sun, which causes an increase in temperature.

The soil thaws, our sleeves shorten, and trees burst forth in bloom. Hens lay more eggs, rabbits start to reproduce like mad, and chicks hatch. The stores fill with these images rendered in marshmallow and chocolate, but you can find the symbols of spring in your garden most readily.

If you do not raise chickens or ducks, see if you can find a local farmer who does. Free-range local eggs return us to the earth; see if you can gather some yourself, especially if you have children. Then gather berries, dandelions, red cabbage, beets, and iris blossoms to form natural dyes; gently boil your dying agent in enough water to cover your berries or leaves, and add a teaspoon of white vinegar per cup of strained dye to help set the color. Boil or empty your eggs by poking a pin-sized hold in one end and a small pea-sized hole in the other, then blow into the pin hole, emptying the contents into a bowl; then dye them outside if it is warm enough. Hang a few in the trees, hide them in the grass, and fill baskets with them in honor of the spring bounty bursting all around.

Hang twine and wool in your trees as a gift to birds forming their nests. Pour a bit of honey and milk on a sacred space to give thanks to the earth. Gently fertilize your early crops—if you planted in protected areas at Imbolc, you should have greens to harvest for a lovely salad. Include some boiled eggs and honey mustard dressing in honor of the return of the warmth.

In warmer climates, you will be able to plant your garden in earnest now. Thank the goddess Ostara for the gifts of the spring, and enjoy the warming days and nights.

Beltane: May 1 in Northern Hemisphere, October 31 in Southern Hemisphere.

Even mainstream culture knows the image of the Maypole, but few elementary schools teach their young students its symbolism. The pole is the phallus of the God, fertilizing the Goddess at this time of planting. We decorate this symbol of fertility and virility with ribbons much like we might a bride, honoring her beauty and power. You can also decorate a pole and wreath with flowers, another timeless symbol of sex, desire, and rebirth.

Leaving freshly picked flowers in a cone or basket upon your neighbors' doors assures their prosperity and creativity in the following year, and they need not even know the meaning of the symbol. Everyone enjoys the surprise of flowers. One can use them everywhere: wear them in your hair, sprinkle yourself with a little rose or violet water, and serve a fresh salad of arugula, violets, and rose petals dressed with your favorite vinaigrette.

Beltane means "bright fire" for another ancient rite, the bonfire. In Irish tradition, on May Eve all fires and candles were extinguished within the home, and a great bonfire was lit in the village square. The great fire burned through the night, and on May Day households could take a sprig of fire from it to light their own hearth fire. Couples who leapt over smaller fires on this day were considered either wed or engaged, and much coupling would occur outside the glow of the great blaze.

Anyone rolling around in the brush had to be careful, though, for on May Eve the fairies come out to play, and one might be whisked away to fairy land in the blink of an eye. Carry a violet on your person to see fairies and a bit of iron in your pocket to keep you safe.

As with all natural celebrations, gather whatever grows in your garden for a feast. With a coldframe, or if you live in a temperate zone, you should have quite a bounty by May Day. If not, this is a good time to plant. Pay attention to nighttime temperatures, though, for some climates can be balmy by day and freezing come nightfall. But certainly some things will be blooming by this date, and a Beltane walk with a loved one beneath flowering fruit trees can be a simple but sweet celebration.

Litha: June 21 in Northern Hemisphere, December 21 in Southern Hemisphere.

The summer solstice, or midsummer, celebrates the height of abundance in the garden. Anna Franklin, in *Midsummer: Magical Celebrations of the Summer Solstice*, writes, "The earth is pregnant with goodness, made fertile by the light of the sun."[101] This is a time of growth and possibility, fertility and joy.

The solstice marks the beginning of Earth's tilt away from the sun and the shortening of days. For this reason, many ancient peoples celebrated the agricultural bounty with fire, a prayer for safety for the crops, the land, and their families. Torches and bonfires mark the land, remembered today with beach fires and barbecues. The Baltic peoples and others in the north honored this change of light with a great bonfire, similar to the Beltane fires that blazed farther south six weeks earlier.

Fire is not only a sign of light, it can be used to cleanse and purify. This is a good holiday to smudge your home and yourself with a bundle of dried sage, sweetgrass, or cedar. If you have aromatic herbs in your yard like kitchen sage and rosemary, throw some on the coals of your grill as well. If you have a fire pit or fireplace, release outdated parts of yourself by burning images or words that represent the aspects you wish to release. Toss a bit of rosemary on the fire at the end to pledge sweetness for your new self and to cleanse the old.

If you can, you may want to sleep outside on Midsummer. Ask your land for its protection that the fairies don't whisk you away or give you nightmares. Lie beneath the moon and stars, sensing the energies beyond our planet to which we are inextricably but subtly connected.

Lammas: August 2 in Northern Hemisphere, February 2 in Southern Hemisphere.

This holy day rests halfway between the summer solstice and the autumn equinox. Days are subtly shortening, but the air is still summery and warm. In many parts of the world these are the "dog days" of summer, when we lie around like tired dogs, drained from the heat. Yet the land promises the first kisses of autumn in yellow leaves and late summer rain.

Often the garden is a wilted mess at this time of the year. You may be harvesting tomatoes and corn, but the cooler-season crops of spinach and carrots have long turned to seed. If the days are not too hot, prepare your garden beds for the next planting of cooler season crops like arugula, mâche, and broccoli. Gather seeds and prepare them for storage. Consider as you harvest, plan, or plant how this time sits poised between seasons. Like much in life, it is a balancing act.

This is a very yang time of year, and you may feel a little strung out. Take time to reconnect with your inner yin, to recharge your batteries by soaking in a forest pond (or imagining your tub rests in the middle of a cool forest) or eating cooling melon. Allow yourself to slow down. Plan a celebration that honors the brightness of the season while welcoming the coming stillness.

Bring to your Lammas celebration any fruits that are ripe, like tomatoes, watermelon, and the first apples. Harvest the corn and last beans. Give thanks to the Corn Goddess for her bounty, and offer some corn to the neighborhood squirrels and raccoons. They may have already helped themselves; let Lammas be a time of truce, honoring that we all must eat and no one owns the earth's bounty. A traditional activity on Lammas is to craft corn dollies out of soaked, dried corn husks.[102] After you've harvested the corn, craft dollies and leave them as offerings for the fairies.

Mabon: About September 21 in Northern Hemisphere, March 21 in Southern Hemisphere.

The autumn equinox marks the poise of light before our descent into winter darkness. This is my favorite time of year, when the deciduous trees prepare for cold by showing their colors, and the air smells of cider and smoke. When I was young, my uncle would host an apple-picking party to harvest the bounty of his two large trees. All the uncles would get good and drunk, the aunts would cook a big feast, and the cousins would try to keep from getting beaned by flying fruit. Other friends of ours took an annual foray into the wild orchards of Vashon Island to pick tart wild apples and host a cider-pressing party. Fresh cider is truly one of the Goddess' most perfect gifts. Tangy and sweet, it reminds me of the precious and tentative nature of life, for it carries the sweet bite of the harvest and the darkening of the year.

Only in autumn can you purchase hard cider on tap, and boxes of apples are readily available at roadside stands and grocery stores alike. Corn husks and scarecrows decorate front porches, everyone bakes a berry-apple pie, and there is always someone trying her hand at winemaking for the first time.

In the midst of the bounty, take time to consider the blessings in your own life. As the light slips toward winter, what have you accomplished this past year? What personal processes are shifting underground now to stew through the winter? What might be rotting in your garden that can be mixed into the compost?

Garden Ritual

Ritual is about creating or honoring change. Your garden can serve as a gathering place for community or private ritual; whether you have a small patio garden or several acres, your garden can be a powerful place to honor life's changes or begin the work of manifestation. Gardens provide gentle reminders of the natural flow of life and our place in it. Ritual is an opportunity for us to reconnect with the places within and around us that remind us of our divine nature. Use ritual to slow down and notice or honor a change in your life, like a death or a beginning. In ritual we notice that the lines between endings and beginnings are blurred, and all is sacred. Ritual can be a formal affair like a wedding or the celebration of a sabbat, or it can be subtle and spontaneous—planting seeds and calling their energies into your garden, sitting quietly in a garden devoted to a specific planet, or brewing a cup of nettle tea.

To design your own ritual, start with the general outline below, adapting as appropriate to focus your energy toward your intended goal. Most rituals include the following sections:

Cleansing

This might be a smudge with smoke, meditating to clear your mind, purging in some way, or bathing. You want to enter sacred space as pure as possible.

Creating Sacred Space

In pagan ritual, a circle is cast to create dedicated safe space to work. In church, the doors are closed. For a wedding, the party walks down the aisle and everyone is seated. An altar helps create sacred space; you may want to set up an altar before or after you purify yourself.

Calling in the Powers You Will Work With

Prayer, invocation, and dedication calls in ancestors, deities, and allies.

Declaration of Intent

"We have gathered here today to witness the marriage..." or stating aloud that a ritual is intended to improve your financial situation are examples of declaring the intent of your ritual.

Raising Energy

Drumming, chanting, dancing, giving a lively sermon—these raise the energy of the ritual's participants.

Directing the Energy

The energy raised from singing or drumming is focused into the intent stated at the beginning of your ritual. In a wedding, the partners exchange rings to formally mark their union. In pagan ritual, a cone of energy is sent into the universe toward the people or situation involved.

Grounding

Any excess energy is released back into the earth. A simple way to do this is by putting your hands on the ground and letting the energy melt away; at church, everyone chants an ending phrase like "and also with you" and then shares tea and cookies.

Exiting Sacred Space and Closure

In pagan ritual, the circle is opened to mark the end

of a ritual. In a wedding, everyone exits the church.

Follow the above outline, adding your own intentions and personal meanings for any ritual you wish to create. When you hold ritual in your garden, invite appropriate allies to participate, and draw on the sacred, natural gifts of the garden for your work. Here are some suggestions:

When You Start a New Garden

Sprinkle some cornmeal at the four directions surrounding your garden, and ask the devas to bless the space. Turn over a spade of earth, and say a prayer for the allies and elements. Take some time to listen to the land and the spirits as they express their wishes and suggestions.

When You Found a Community Garden Space

In addition to blessings and prayers, share a meal in the space made by community members. Invite people to share their vision for the space.

For Handfastings or Weddings

Make decorations out of seasonal flowers, vines, and even stones. Ask the devas to bless your work as your consecrate the space for the ritual union. Make some element of the ritual out of materials from your garden space, like a broom, Jewish wedding *huppah*, or arbor.

For Births and Naming Ceremonies

Ask the spirits for the best place to bless this new person. The night before, leave a bowl of water in this space to be cleansed by the moon; use this water in your ritual.

When You Begin a New Job
Ask for guidance and blessings for your new path. Ask for a gift from the garden to keep you grounded at work, like a stone or a seed head. Put this gift on your desk or in your locker where you will see it daily.

When It Is Time to Let Go of a Job, Person, or Experience
Bury or burn a talisman of this loss in your garden, and ask the universe to help you grieve, let go, and heal.

When You Need a Change in Your Finances
The garden is all about bounty and wealth; spend some time aligning with these powers so that they may bless other areas in your life. Give thanks to the garden by pouring milk, wine, honey, or another sacred substance on the earth.

For the Sabbats and Esbats (Full Moons)
See "The Wheel of the Year" section above for ideas of how to celebrate the eight holy days in your garden. New and full moon ceremonies can be as simple as a prayer beneath the moon to give thanks and ask for blessings, or as elaborate as an all-out pagan hoopla. For suggestions, see Phyllis Curott's *Witchcrafting*; on pages 132–139 she describes rituals for new, full, and waning moon cycles.

When a Girl Begins Her Moon Blood or a Woman Ends Hers
Lie on the earth. Let the earth bless you during this powerful time of change. Listen to her for messages about your life. Bury something at the base of

a favorite tree or other spot to mark a letting go of the past and a welcoming of the new. Pour some moon blood on your garden, or sprinkle the ground with tears if you feel grief. Your regular moon blood can also be used as an offering, and you can use this monthly time to reconnect with the Goddess and the ground.

When You Need Strength as You Create a New World

The garden is a tool for change, but it can also be a respite and an inspiration. Spend time doing nothing in your garden to align with the immense power of creativity and generation held there. When you face challenges in life as a sacred sister, bathe in the blessings of the garden to renew and realign with your deepest intentions.

Sacred Sister: Wangari Maathai

activist

The first African woman to win the Nobel Peace Prize, Maathai teaches us about living one's convictions no matter what the odds. Born in 1940 in Nyeri, Kenya, she grew up the daughter of subsistence farmers. She became the first African woman to receive a doctorate degree, which she obtained from the University of Nairobi, where she also taught veterinary anatomy. In 1977 she founded the Green Belt Movement (GBM), an organization run mostly by poor, rural women dedicated to planting millions of trees in an effort to reverse deforestation and desertification.[103] "It took me a lot of days and nights to convince people that women could improve their environment without much technology or without much financial resources," she said on BBC's *Africa Live*.[104] She stuck with her efforts, and GBM has been very successful.

Despite people's disbelief in their own power, and against major, often violent resistance from corrupt governments and the former dictator Moi, in thirty years GBM has planted over 30 million trees and provided jobs for more than 100,000 people, mostly women.[105] The Movement has spread to other African nations as well.

In an address to the UN, Maathai said, "For the last thirty years, governments have called the environment and women's rights 'emerging issues.' How can that be when 70 percent of the world's poorest people are women, and 50 percent of them depend for their subsistence on the use of natural resources?"[106] She sees a strong connection among many international issues, from AIDS to poverty to deforestation, linking them to scarcity of resources and the need for justice among the poor. She faces them all with immense courage and conviction. For her efforts, she has won numerous awards worldwide and been granted four honorary doctoral degrees.

She says, "Sometimes I've had difficult times, and I think having those and overcoming them for women is very important—you don't have to be down and out. You can get back up."[107] No matter what you face, your fire can be found within. Remember Maathai as you work to rebirth your life and the world. Her warm hug, her glowing smile, and her beautiful, earthy hands can be a guide for all women to find their true strength and beauty and live it each and every day.

Fire Meditation: Finding Your Passion

As you walk the path of the sacred land, you will feel a need to not only do healing and transformation in yourself, but in the world as well. This magical work of manifestation will grow naturally out of your own inner fire. You may have banked this fire within for a long time. It still smolders away inside, and it is time to fan the fire and unleash the power within. Remember that a forest fire can be started by a single spark.

To reclaim the passion within you and begin to be the transformation you seek, start with a meditation and ritual on your inner fire. Find a comfortable place to sit where you will not be interrupted for twenty minutes to an hour. Outside in your garden is best, but anywhere you feel safe and protected will do. You can close your eyes if you prefer, or let them rest with a soft focus a few feet in front of you. Take a few deep, cleansing breaths. Let the distractions of your day settle like stones in a pond. Let the ripples on the pond's surface calm. Your thoughts are now like leaves floating on the surface. Let them float by, focusing on none of them.

When you feel calm and centered, close your eyes. In your mind, see yourself walking down a dirt path. The land around you is dry and plain. Ahead of you rises a red stone wall. The path leads you to a gate, which you push open. As you step over the threshold into a walled garden, you are greeted with a moist breeze that reminds you of jasmine and cinnamon. Your feet press into moist, springy moss. You enter this walled garden and close the gate behind you.

Once the door is closed, the wall disappears and you find yourself in a huge garden that spreads beyond the farthest point you can see. Bright tropical flowers grow next to vibrant tomato plants and vigorous pumpkin vines. Great climbing roses cascade over archways that lead you to sweet shaded groves and shimmering ponds. Take a few moments to explore this fantastic garden.

After exploring for as long as you like, you come to the edge of a clear blue lake. Undress and enter the water, which is refreshing yet warm enough for comfort. Dive in, letting the water cleanse you inside and out. As you swim, you see images of how you have let your passions and creative expression be stifled. Let any memories or feelings that arise float away and be cleansed by the magical lake. Take as long as you need.

When you feel lighter and refreshed, return to shore. Watch the water drip off your glistening skin. Admire the beautiful curve of your thighs, the soft mound of hair between your legs, the roundness of your breasts. Feel your feet firmly planted on the earth, and feel the gentle but powerful pulse of the Mother beneath you.

You look up to discover before you the most beautiful woman you have ever seen. Her shining hair hangs to her wide hips, her round breasts hang full. She glows with an inner light, and she smiles to see you.

"Hello," she says, greeting you by name. "I am Eve, first woman, Goddess of the Tree of Life. Know that you have been cleansed by the Lake of the Mother; you are now ready to draw on your passion to create the world anew. I will help you walk this path of power." She shares with you a chant to help you awaken the creative fires within.

I reclaim my fire, my passion.
The pleasure and the pain
that make me whole,
the light and the dark
that burn within,
the power of creation
and destruction that are
granted me by the Goddess:
I reclaim these powers.
I reclaim these powers.
I reclaim these powers.

Sit for as long as you need with this chant and any sensations or feelings that arise.

Repeat this chant as many times as you like. When you are ready, say goodbye to the goddess Eve and turn to head out of the garden.

Walk along a path that leads you uphill and into a swirling fog. Return to your body, sitting in meditation. Open your eyes, wiggle your fingers and toes, and take deep breaths to return you to your physical being. Feel the energy inside your body, the pulse of your heartbeat and the tingle of Being. When you are ready, rise and go eat or drink something to get you fully back into yourself. Record your meditation images and insights in your journal.

What did you discover about your passions? What sparks lie inside, aching to germinate beneath the warmth of the sun?

Fire Magic: Seed Saving

During the fire time of the year, late summer, plants who were not harvested produce seed heads. Some of these we eat, like corn, while others we regard as a nuisance, like dandelion fuzz. The ecologically conscious gardener saves some of her seeds for replanting, participating in the thousand-year-old lineage of seeds.

Saving seeds is ecologically responsible for several reasons. First, most seeds in the United States, Canada, and the Untied Kingdom are not organic. They are treated with fungicides and other chemicals to assure their viability, uniformity, and even dependence on fertilizers and other chemicals. Many seed companies in the United States are owned by fertilizer companies, which are actually petroleum companies. Buying organic seeds and saving seeds from your organically grown plants reduces our reliance on and use of petroleum products. These practices reduce the amount of poisons going into the earth. Even though you may only plant five seeds one season, multiplied by 68 million home gardeners and agricultural uses adds up to a lot of treated seed.

Second, the seeds sold by agribusiness seed companies tend toward monoculture: we grow one or two kinds of corn, one kind of pea, one kind of broccoli, and so on, despite there being a huge range of climates in the continental U.S. alone and several thousand edible plants on Earth. These basic types found in most seed displays are not necessarily the most nutritious varieties; they are simply those that produce the largest crop that is most conducive to mechanical harvest and long-distance shipping. It does not matter that the home gardener needs relatively small crops that travel no farther than her kitchen; agribusiness is interested in high yield and market domination. By selling and growing a limited variety, we put ourselves at risk for food-crippling blights. Developing your own varieties that do well in your climate, or supporting small seed companies that do this work for you, greatly reduces the risk of losing an entire variety of food.

An unknown number of plant varieties have disappeared because those who developed them and painstakingly saved the seeds found no one to continue their work. Seed saving is good ecological practice because it protects biodiversity, crucial not just for our food supply but for the health of the planet. A seed's lineage goes back thousands of years, mother plant to mother plant. When no one saves a plant's seed or only hybrid varieties are grown, a rich history comes to an end. Many of the plants you buy in your average nursery are hybrids, plants that will not reproduce true to form. A plant that will produce offspring like the parent is known as an heirloom.

The offspring of two parent plants, hybrids will not reproduce true to form—you never know what you will get. If you want to grow the same variety of plant year to year, you need to repurchase seed from the company. Nationally available hybrid-type seeds are not necessarily well adapted to one's climate and do not represent anywhere near the variety of plants one can grow at home. Some hybrid seeds are even sterile, or produce plants that are "seedless." While this may be a convenience when you bite into a watermelon, a seedless plant is a biological dead end.

Dead-end plants mean reliance on seed makers. Since we need seeds to grow food, it follows that whoever controls the seed stock controls the people. They control the types of food available to the people. A third powerful reason to save seed: we can regain control over our food sources by supporting companies that sell heirloom organic seeds and by saving our own.

Seed saving is advanced gardening, but like any gardening technique, it can become second nature once you get the basic idea. Most gardening books include very little information, if any, on how to save seeds, but seed saving lets you take back your power as a sacred sister while protecting the health of the planet.

In order to save your seeds, you first need to produce seeds worth saving—that is, fertile seeds. Seeds are the female parts of the plant that have been fertilized by the male part, or the pollen. This occurs in one of three ways: by wind, animals, or the plant itself. A plant must be fertilized with pollen from the same variety in order to reproduce baby plants the same as their parents, or true to type. To assure this occurs, plants that are wind pollinated, like corn, beets, and spinach, must be at least a mile away from other varieties or their reproductive parts covered with bags or cages. Insect-pollinated plants, like carrots, cucumber, and parsley, must be grown at least a quarter mile from other varieties if not covered. Self-pollinating plants only need to be a few rows away from other varieties; these are pollinated right within the plant's flowers, and the distance is simply to assure that any escaping pollen from one variety does not result in cross-pollination. This last variety includes beans, lettuce, peas, peppers, and tomatoes, and offers the best place for a novice seed saver to learn this practice. I will explain how to save seed from these four plants; if you wish to learn more about seed saving or learn how to save seeds from other plants, please see Suzanne Ashworth's comprehensive guide *Seed to Seed*.

Check your seed packet to make sure it says heirloom or F2; you will not want to save seed from F1 hybrids. These will not produce true to form, and may even produce sterile seeds. Choose several of your more vigorous plants for seed saving; look for plants that bear heavily and appear true to type. Plants that are small or produce off-type flowers or fruits should be removed, tossed into the compost before flowering. You want to avoid the pollen from this plant fertilizing any of the seeds you will save. Gather seeds from several plants to avoid inbreeding.

Let pod plants, like peas and beans, dry on the vine, and remove the seeds from the pod when fully dry. To make sure the seeds are fully dry, smash a few with a hammer; if they shatter, they are fully dry. Freeze the dry seeds for five days to kill off any bean weevil eggs that might be present. When you remove the container of seeds from the freezer, let it sit overnight to come to room temperature to avoid the formation of condensation on the cold seeds. Then store the seeds in a cool, dry, dark location until next planting.

Pepper seeds are relatively easy to save as well. Grow different pepper varieties at least five hundred feet apart or cover plants with a mesh cage to avoid cross-pollination. Thump or rub the flowers between 7 and 11 AM to encourage pollination. Peppers are self-pollinating, but sometimes require a nudge from wind, insects, or humans to dust the inside of the flower with its own pollen. Early morning is best because of cool temperatures mixed with plenty of light. When the fruit is fully mature, cut open the pepper, leaving the stem attached to the core. Take care to not damage the core when removing the flesh. If you aren't ready to eat the peppers, store the fruit in plastic containers in the refrigerator or roast them on the grill and freeze for later use. When working with hot peppers, wear thick rubber gloves and work in a well-ventilated area. Dry pepper seeds on a screen or ceramic plate away from direct sunlight until the seeds break when folded. Store in a cool, dry, dark location; plant within three years.

To save tomato seeds, pick fully ripe fruit and slice across the middle. Squeeze the seeds and gel into a bucket. Set aside the container for a few days to allow the mixture to ferment, a process that kills seed-borne tomato diseases and removes the gelatinous sack surrounding each seed. Stir the mixture twice a day. Store the container outside the house and out of reach of animals or children, for the mixture will become quite smelly. When bubbles can be seen rising in the mixture or a layer of mold completely covers the surface, the fermentation process is complete. Do not let it sit longer or the seeds may begin to germinate. Add enough water to double the fermented mixture, and stir vigorously. The good seeds will settle, and the immature seeds and mold will rise to the surface; pour off the unwanted debris and repeat the process until you have good seeds at the bottom of your bucket. Strain the seeds, wipe the strainer on a towel to remove as much moisture as possible, and dry your seeds on a screen or a ceramic dish out of direct sunlight, stirring twice a day to hasten drying.

You can eat your lettuce and save the seed, too. Pick off outer lettuce leaves as they become large enough to eat, but leave the plant in the ground. When the weather warms, allow the lettuce to grow a seed head. It will form florets, which will all open on the same day. After self-pollinating, the florets will close. The florets are not open very long, so the risk of cross-pollination is slim. However, to be certain, separate your lettuce varieties by at least twelve feet or cage them as they open. Lettuce seeds are ready for harvest 12–24 days after flowering; during that period, shake the seed heads into a large paper sack, and store the sack in a cool, dark location.

Pour the gathered seeds onto a fine mesh screen that allows the seed to fall through while separating out the chaff and lettuce feathers. Gently shake the screen while blowing softly over the top to blow off the chaff. Store the seed in a cool, dry location for up to three years in a paper or wax bag or a plastic or metal container, like an old, clean yogurt cup with a lid or a film canister.

Seed saving can start as an experiment and result in a full-blown obsession, especially if the plants growing in your garden start to exhibit particularly desired characteristics. Share your bounty and your knowledge with others to revive this dying art that is so crucial to the future of our food, our gardens, and our planet. For more information on seed saving, see Fire Resources.

Fire Resources

Suggested Herbals

My two favorite herbals are:

Rosemary Gladstar's Family Herbal by Rosemary Gladstar (Storey Books, 2001)

The New Holistic Herbal by David Hoffman (Barnes and Noble Books, 1990)

Herbs

For information on at-risk medicinal herbs, see *Planting the Future,* edited by Rosemary Gladstar and Pamela Hirsch. Or contact:

United Plant Savers
P.O. Box 98
East Barre, VT 05649
www.unitedplantsavers.org

To learn more about native plants in your area, contact the National Wildlife Federation:

NWF
11100 Wildlife Center Drive
Reston, VA 20190-5362
(800) 822-9919

For a state-by-state guide of native plants, see their online database at www.enature.com/native__invasive/natives.asp. Keep in mind that different parts of a given state will have different climates and therefore support different natives.

Organic Seeds

Seeds of Change
seedsofchange.com
(888) 762-7333

Offers a free catalog of their unique organic seeds, books, and foods. A free online newsletter is also available, with articles about seed saving, organic agriculture, and permaculture.

Sow Organic Seed
P.O. Box 527
Williams OR 97544
(888) 709-7333
www.organicseed.com

Offers organic seed, a newsletter, and a wealth of online articles.

High Mowing Seeds
76 Quarry Road
Wolcott, VT 05680
(802) 472-6174
Fax (802) 472-3201
www.highmowingseeds.com

An independent, family-owned business dedicated to supporting sustainable agriculture. Offers open-pollinated, heirloom, and hybrid organic seeds, including vegetables, herbs, and flowers, as well as a selection of books.

Seed Saving

See Suzanne Ashworth's *Seed to Seed* (Seed Saver Publications, 1991) for a wealth of information on plants, seeds, and seed saving. Chapter 6 of *Gardening for the Future of the Earth* by Shapiro and Harrison (Bantam Books,

2000) has a great "Beginner's Two-Minute Drill for Seed Saving." This book also includes a chapter on plant breeding, if you wish to take your seed saving a step further.

International Seed Saving Institute
P.O. Box 4619
Ketchum, ID 83340
www.seedsave.org
Offers online information about seed saving as well as books and other resources.

Seed Savers Exchange
3094 North Winn Road
Decorah, IA 52101
(563) 382-5990
Fax (563) 382-5872
www.seedsavers.org
Offers a large variety of heirloom seeds, books (including information on seed saving), gifts, and information on their visitor's center and organization membership.

Native Seed/SEARCH
526 N. 4th Ave.
Tucson, AZ 85705-8450
Toll-free (866) 622-5561
Fax (520) 622-5591
www.nativeseeds.org
A nonprofit organization preserving crop seeds that connect Native American cultures to their land. They sell seeds and gifts, including Native crafts, books, and videos. They also have a large seed bank, a promise to the cultural and ecological future of the Southwest.

Mother Earth News Issue #107, Sept/Oct 1997 published an article about seed saving. It can be found online at www.motherearthnews.com/top__articles/1987__September__October/Saving__Seeds.

NOTES

CHAPTER 4

Water

it's a deep blue sea

it's a bottomless swim

it's the sparkle in the eye

of your most beautiful friend

it's the inkling of doubt

'bout where you end & begin

it's a deep blue sea ...

Tony Edelblute,
"No Name Thing"

The Living Sheath

When we face the west, we face the land where the sun dips below the sea and calls us into dreamland. In the west live our hopes for the future, all our dreams and wishes that swim in the salty subconscious. In the west we find the element water, a crucial element for gardening and for all of life. Our planet is called Earth, but two thirds of her surface is covered in water. "The oceans, lakes and rivers of the world are connected by water vapor in the atmosphere, creating a huge, living sheath within which all life finds its home," writes Anna Bond.[108] We live in a womb of water.

Water is about relationship, the interconnection of all life via this fascinating and elusive being that is so much more than just bonded hydrogen and oxygen. Scientists believe that life began on the planet when lightning interacted with Earth's early atmosphere, which consisted mostly of water and water vapor. This union created amino acids, the building blocks of life as we know it. Water makes life on Earth possible.

Water is in constant motion, even when still to our eyes. Water's microscopic layers continuously slide over each other like the layers of an onion in motion. "Water by its essential nature is always moving, and by constantly moving it serves to create, protect, energize, nourish, and sustain life,"writes William Marks in *The Holy Order of Water.*[109]

Consider for a moment the flow of water from sea to sky, sky to soil, soil to tree ... water evaporates into the atmosphere, surrounding the planet in water vapor. The human body participates in this cycle as well: your brain needs water to think, to plan and dream. Your liver needs water to filter blood and toxins. Your skin needs water to interact effectively with the environment. What your body cannot use, or whatever water is needed to flush waste products, leaves the body and reenters the cycle. It is cleaned and recycled by more water and microorganisms, and used to hydrate fields, replenish rivers, and give life to the planet.

Water is a crucial element for any garden, whether you grow hydroponic tomatoes or cactus in sand. Taking time to know water more deeply may change the way you approach the garden—and certainly will give you food for thought about life on Earth and the sacred nature of water.

Water Meditation

Pour a glass of water and sit in a quiet space where you will not be disturbed. Hold the glass in your hands and close your eyes. Feel your hip bones on the ground or chair. Become aware of the earth beneath you. Now bring your attention to your breath moving in and out of your lungs. Listen to your heartbeat. Spend a few moments paying attention to your body and the present moment.

Now shift your focus, the same awareness you gave to your breath, to the water in the glass. Let your body be aware of the water, not just your mind. Feel it. In your heart's eye, see it. Listen to it deeply. Allow your awareness to sink more and more deeply into the substance in the glass you hold in your hands.

Become aware of the water in your own body, the water in the earth beneath you and the air around you, in your house's pipes and in bodies of water nearby. How do these sources relate to the water in the glass? In what ways do they feel different or the same?

The water in your body, in the air around you, in the glass, and in the planet's rivers and oceans is all one continuous sphere, a great dance of water enlivening the planet. Sit with this image or feeling for several minutes, simply breathing water, being water, being in water.

You may also want to take a bath at this time with new understanding of the medium of water and its own intelligence. You can salt the water for a cleansing ritual, or soak in fresh water for clarity. When you drain the bath, release old ways of seeing water and give thanks for the gifts you have received.

Spend as much time as you like exploring the essence and energy of water. The first time you do this you might not feel a lot, but as you spend more time with water you will discover some powerful and surprising realities about its nature. Repeat this meditation as many times as you like to fully understand the essence of water. Draw or write in your journal whatever you discovered and any questions or dreamlike images that arose.

Water Allies: Undines & Naiads

An immortal water spirit, the undine fell deeply in love with a human man. When she married him and birthed his child, she gained a soul, inheriting both the joy and pain of mortality (not to mention motherhood). The undine's story is a metaphor for how water takes on the form of its container and of any energy it contacts. It teaches us that love brings both great joy and sorrow. When we lose those we love, we shed an undine's tears.

The undine's cousin, the naiad, is a nymph who watches over springs and rivers. Her name comes from the Greek words for "running water" and "to flow." Her sisters preside over other water aspects as well: the Nereid over the Mediterranean, the Oceanids over the sea, and Limneads over lakes, marshes, and swamps. In ancient Greece, all nymphs were worshiped at a *nymphaeum*, a large fountain raised near a well. Nymphs were said to bring humans enhanced fertility and healthy growth.

The water over which a naiad presides is thought to have powers of healing, inspiration, or prophecy. If that water dries up, the naiad perishes, for she is intimately connected with her element. Of course, humans and the planet share this connection; when our fresh water is gone or polluted, we too will die.

In Slavic nations, the water deities are known as *rusalki*. Dangerous and mischievous, they nonetheless bring abundance and good crops. The people tossed *morena*, "death dolls," into the river each spring as a symbol of the end of death-bringing winter and an offering to the rusalki—with hopes that the dolls would be enough sacrifice that no human lives would be taken by the dangerously rising waters.[110] Rusalki offer another lesson of the essential yet potentially destructive nature of water.

Water elementals teach us to watch and learn, to float in the cool depths before acting. They teach us about flow, about being flexible but loyal. Sometimes their loyalty can get the best of them, for they possess a tendency for jealousy. If you too tend to feel jealous about people or things, remember that we are all one in spirit and in water. As long as we keep the flow going, we will all have more than we need. Jealousy only blocks the flow. Sit by a running stream to understand better how to let your heart be open.

Call on an undine or naiad to watch over your garden faucet and any water feature in your yard. If you have a bird bath, tend it well and do not allow it to dry up. As you water your plants, ask the nymphs to bless and protect your garden. They will happily dance through your veggies and trees, fulfilling their roles as protectors of the natural world.

GODDESS

YEMAYA

THIS EBONY-SKINNED Momma Ocean protects women and children, and she understands a woman's desire to create and nurture. She herself birthed Earth's waters, as well as all the gods and goddesses.

Whether you long to create a lush and nourishing garden, a work of art, or a child, call on Yemaya's sweet and powerful blessings. Offer her corn and yams beneath the full moon, or dance in your birthday suit at the edge of the ocean. In exchange, offer her a promise you can keep that will help protect the planet's water, like donating to an environmental activist organization or cleaning up a local stream or beach.

Water Meditation: Life Dreams

In visioning your garden in the east and dancing with Eve in the south, what dreams about your life have surfaced? The gifts of water include dreams and deep emotions; while swimming through the watery depth, the boundaries dissolve between your dream life and who you currently are. "Water melts the walls we have created that block the flow of our emotions, which, like the rains from heaven, nourish the landscape of our lives so that our dreams can grow wild and fruitful," writes Phyllis Curott.[111] Offer these seedling dreams to the Mother Ocean and her sweet rains to encourage them to germinate and grow strong. Dream seeds have a long dormancy period; they can last for hundreds of years. All they need is the heat of passion and the wetness of nurturing love to emerge and bear fruit.

Take a few moments to swim with your dreams and share them with Yemaya through the following meditation.

Close your eyes and breathe deeply. Listen to your heartbeat. Picture yourself at the beach by the ocean. You are wearing nothing, and no one is around. You approach the water and wade in until it reaches your waist, then you dive into the water. You can breathe under water, and you swim smoothly into the cool depths. Sunlight dances in beautiful, shimmering waves over your skin. You are perfectly safe and feel at home in the water.

Ahead of you rises a sandy underwater hill. You swim up to the hill and grasp onto strong seaweed strands to keep you stationary as you gaze out into the darkness of the deep sea. Though the vastness feels somewhat overwhelming, you feel completely safe. You feel the loving presence of the Mother all around you.

With your thoughts, you send to the Mother's depths a question: "What is my secret dream? What am I here on Earth to do?" Before you an image appears, as if you were gazing upon a three-dimensional film screen. Fuzzy at first, it becomes clear to you after a moment. Watch the images that Yemaya shares with you, the images that portray your life path and your deepest dreams.

When the images shimmer off into watery sunlight, thank the Mother and swim back to shore. Emerge from the water, letting the sea drip from your skin.

When you are ready, come back into awareness of your heartbeat, your breath, the weight of your body. Open your eyes and sit or stand up. Stretch and shake your body to bring you fully back. Record in your journal what you learned, what Mother Ocean reminded you, in words and pictures.

Next, write in your journal how you can water these dreams to help them grow. What further clarity do you need? What training do you need? Who do you know who can help you get on the right path? You need not figure everything out now. This is a place to record your thoughts, dreams, fears, and plans. Realizing these dreams may take time. Keep bringing them to light by talking about them, writing them down, and drawing their symbols and images. They will come to pass.

I look back at journals from my junior-high school days, when I wanted to be a writer. I read my journals from high school, when I dreamed of the perfect partner. In journals written in college and after I graduated, I find my ideas for my healing career. When I recorded these dreams they felt both very real and very far away. Today, actually not so long from that time, I practice spiritual healing work and I write. I am married to a sweet man I consider my life companion, and we have a beautiful baby daughter. The path to this time has felt long, and my triumphs have felt small. Yet here I am. That you read these words proves that dedication to a dream yields fruit.

When you feel discouraged or alone, turn to Mother Water to find cleansing and support. She can be found in the salty tears of the ocean or the clear sparkle of a mountain stream. Call to her, and she is there.

The Ethic of Water

Sacred gardening approaches life from both inner spiritual work and practical action in the world. Inner work, including meditation, journeying, and personal growth, influences and guides the work you do in the world. Throughout this book you have seen how spiritual perspectives inform how you garden. One area that illustrates this most keenly is in regard to water.

Humans use over half of the planet's fresh water for our needs and desires. Much of that water use is extremely sloppy and wasteful, like overhead spraying of agricultural fields in arid climates. Water runoff is nearly always polluted with chemicals and petroleum products, and as we suck aquifers dry, we drastically increase the concentration of pollutants in these underground wells of fresh water. In 2003, one fifth of all freshwater species were threatened or extinct because of pollution, habitat destruction, and water diversion. Half of the planet's wetlands have been destroyed. Dams, the diversion of water for electricity, irrigation, and drinking water, drastically alter freshwater habitats, leading to massive habitat destruction.[112] Not only is this destruction heartbreaking in itself, it carries a dramatic punch line: by destroying the planet's biodiversity, we destroy our only home. Hogging water and other resources ultimately will bring about our own destruction.

We all share the planet's fresh water, the same water the planet had when one third of today's human population called Earth home. When I taught outdoor education to sixth-grade students, during the Water Station I would ask everyone to take a big swig of water, then ask them what they had just consumed. I told them that it was, in fact, dinosaur urine. After the laughter and groans settled, we discussed how all the fresh water on the planet is recycled and finite. What the dinosaurs drank, we drink. What our neighbor flushed down the toilet yesterday is cleaned and recycled to our faucet in a few months or years.

Water is the universal solvent, which is why it can be constantly recycled. However, we have added to our water so many chemicals, both intentionally and unintentionally, that the water we drink is actually very different from the water the dinosaurs or even our grandparents drank. We may have fewer disease-causing microbes in our water, but we also consume with a glass or absorb in the shower lead, arsenic, fuel oxygenates, radon, prescription medicines—the list goes on. Because water is such a powerful solvent, it will take on and carry almost anything we give it.

We think of water as being H_2O, two hydrogen molecules bound to a single oxygen molecule. This chemical structure is only true, however, as water vapor; water in the form we drink or swim and bathe in is highly variable. It will take on anything it comes in contact with: chemicals, pollutants, even words and images. Dr. Masaru Emoto of Japan photographed water crystals under high magnification from different sources around the world, including pure mountain springs and highly polluted rivers, to see how they differed. He then photographed crystals before and after certain words, phrases, or photographs were attached to the water's container. Water exposed to the word *love* looks a lot like the crystals from pure mountain streams,[113] while the same water exposed to "You make me sick" resembles crystals from heavily polluted water.[114] Clean love water creates clear, beautiful crystals, while polluted crystals look sludgy and brown.[115]

Animals and plants are made mostly of water, and the water molecules in our bodies take on the energy they contact. Loved children grow strong and vital, while abused people become sluggish and dark; the same is true in the garden. The plants in our gardens are highly sensitive to the kind of water they receive. By understanding water more deeply you will be able to offer yourself, your garden, and your planet more powerful and healthful nurturing. As water researcher Jennifer Greene said, "With water we are always moving back and forth between the worlds of the spirit and the senses. If we become students of water, of the wateriness of water, the very nature of water, we will learn a new social ethic."[116]

Our Relationship with Water

Every gardener is familiar with her plants' needs for water, but few of us consider exactly where that water comes from, where it goes, and what plants actually do with it. I highly recommend touring your local water treatment plant and learning about your local watershed. When the rain falls in your area, which way does it slide down nearby mountains? Which rivers and lakes fill with that rain? How does it reach you? What particulates are in your water and why? Many of us learned the evaporation-condensation-precipitation cycle in elementary school, but few of us know specifics about the water moving through our own homes. Visiting a local treatment plant, reservoir, or river in your watershed will deepen your relationship with the water that comes out of your tap, the water that supplements rain to nourish your garden's plants. Consider organizing a fieldtrip for your neighborhood, community center, or child's classroom to the local treatment plant, reservoirs, and other parts of the local water system so others can also become more aware of this precious resource.

After learning more about the water in your own home, look at ways you can use it and interact with it in greater consciousness. Sandra Postel and Brian Richter write in *Rivers for Life* that we humans need to learn to adapt to Mother Nature rather than always trying to force water out of a stone: "What this means from a practical standpoint is that instead of planning to make every year as good as it can be for us [humans], we plan instead to share the hardship of water-deficient years and the surplus of water-abundant years with the natural communities around us."[117] In other words, we must consciously participate in the greater relationship of water.

In the garden, irrigation comes from two sources: weather and plumbing. Both are results of complex relationships. "All weather is mainly the result of water's interaction with the powers of the sun, the spin of the earth, the pull of the moon, the flow of ocean currents, and the motion of atmospheric winds," reminds William Marks in *The Holy Order of Water.*[118] Our plumbing is a mostly unseen matrix connecting us to our local water service station, reservoirs, and sewage treatment system. These complex relationships make it possible to grow a garden, for plants need water to grow and thrive.

Plants need water for growth, nutrition, and structure. Initially, water helps to soften the seed coat of a plant, and it then serves three main purposes in a plant's growth. Water makes up about 70 percent of a plant, carrying nutrients and minerals from the roots to the plant's body. It gives the plant electrons necessary to synthesize the sun's energy into food. It also gives it form by filling out the plant's cells.

The electrostatic nature of water, the property that gives water its surface tension, makes it possible for plants to grow tall. A tree's height is actually limited by the water's own weight pulling on itself; above about 420 feet, the molecules in the xylem become too weighted down by the water molecules below them to move. Without moving water, the leaves cannot photosynthesize.[119]

While working in your garden, from soil to seeds to harvest, hold the role of water in your consciousness. Listen to the water in trees, corn stalks, and pea tendrils. Remember the squirrels, ground water, and honey bees as you utilize water throughout the day to bathe, drink, or water the garden beds. Ask yourself what a new social ethic of water might look like. How would our world be different if based on the ethic of water?

Natural Pest Control

A major source of water pollution is non-point source pollution (NPS), which means there is no single point, or source, of the pollution, like a paper mill dumping waste. Gardeners can reduce NPS by reducing the use of fertilizers, pesticides, and other household chemicals. All chemicals used in the home should be applied and disposed of responsibly. I discussed fertilizer use in chapter 1: Earth; now I will discuss ways to use little or no pesticides.

Sometimes a pest is in the eye of the beholder. Wasps, for instance, are rarely detrimental, and in fact they help the gardener by eating insects that eat your plants. A wasp sting is quite rare. When I had a pond, wasps would spend time drinking and basking on the water while I weeded around the pond or cleaned the filter. I was never bothered by them. Ants, too, tend to be annoying in the house but in the garden are beneficial. Most garden bugs can be left alone with no damage to your plants.

Sometimes, however, a plant will be covered in aphids, leaf borers, mites, or another insect that will consume the entire plant. When this happens it is always because of an imbalance. A healthy plant deters pests. The problem lies not with the insects, but with the plant's soil or other growing conditions. In the case of plagues of insects, the imbalance occurs on a larger scale, usually affecting an entire region. In both cases, applying a chemical fertilizer only increases the imbalance.

The first step, then, in dealing with garden pests, is to nourish the plant. Top dress the entire affected bed and surrounding areas with compost. Take a soil test and apply small amounts of needed nutrients. Cover scorched plants with shade cloth, or move pale plants to a sunnier location. Water more deeply or less frequently, as needed. If none of these approaches works, talk to the plant to ask it why it is unhappy.

Next, talk to the pest itself. Explain that these plants are grown for the nourishment or enjoyment of your family, and while you are willing to share some, you want to save the plant. Offer one plant in a row to the pests. They may all move to that one plant, which you will leave solely for them. If you have a large garden, offer a whole section, which you can leave wild and let the bugs go at it.

However, if you have a small garden with only a few plants, you can apply natural pesticides in moderation. I never use anything stronger than garlic tea (a head of garlic boiled in two quarts of water, cooled) or soapy water (about a tablespoon of phosphate-free liquid soap in an average spray bottle of water). For larger pests like squirrels, try hot pepper spray, available at garden stores. Do not use hot pepper spray if you have small children exploring the garden. Deer can be deterred through the use of taste repellents such as hot pepper spray, soapy water, rotten eggs, and scented deterrents like scented soaps, garlic, and fabric softener.[120] Cover berries and gourds with wire cages or bird netting to keep squirrels, birds, and deer from munching your fruits.

Finally, keep in mind that garden pests are just living their lives, making their homes and finding food, just like you. We can perhaps use their sharing of our food as a lesson in community. I get so frustrated with the squirrels who live in our yard, but I respect that we are sharing space. They like it here. Free food, five trees to live and play in, and no predators (my cats ignore them). They don't see that digging holes in the fluffy compost and mulch means death to my seedlings or seeds. Last spring I had a talk with them and explained that this garden was to grow food for my family. I was happy to share some of it with them, but they had to give it a chance to grow first. In exchange for their staying out of the beds, I would leave them nuts or corn. They could dig holes in the mulch and in the yards, but not in my garden.

They agreed for a while, at least as evidenced by the lack of holes in my beds. To be safe, I covered the beds with bird netting to slow them down a little.

Then I began seeing holes in the beds. They killed a baby kale plant. Then they dug around in a flat of germinating seeds I had set out in the sun. I was furious, but still committed to sharing the space. So I just kept asking them to stay out and chased them out of the beds. And scowled.

Then one day I was turning compost and came across the abandoned squirrel nest I had tossed in the pile a few weeks back. It had been lined with squirrel fur. I discovered while pulling it apart that the fur had been attached to a whole squirrel, who had apparently died in her sleep. The squirrels had simply tossed the entire nest, dead friend and all, out of their tree and built a new nest. I had placed the old nest in my compost pile.

I could hardly be mad at them after that. One of their dead was now nourishing my compost pile and would subsequently nourish my garden and my family. Somehow that seemed pretty fair.

I saw a squirrel the other day fighting a stick, flipping around like a puppy with a ball. They leap like superheroes from tree to tree and rival any tightrope walker on the electrical wires. I cannot help but laugh. They continue to baffle and frustrate me, chomping on my pumpkins and squash and eating all the strawberries while the fruits are still green. They remind me, though, to lighten up in the midst of all of my Very Important Work as a gardener, writer, activist, and mother. When plagued by a determined garden pest, ask yourself what lesson it offers you. How can you slow down and open to the language of the land?

The sacred land includes all of our relations. Sometimes that means sharing, whether we share corn, squash, or water. We are but one part of a whole and need to keep that whole in mind when facing garden "pests."

Flow Forms: The Shape of Water

Water always seeks to form a perfect sphere, the most energetically efficient shape in the cosmos. On Earth it encounters various forces like gravity that push or pull against this urge. When water encounters these forces, it forms spirals and vortices—picture water vapor, or steam, rising from a cup of tea, or a drop of food coloring in a glass of clear water. These shapes are always present in moving water. Since water is so crucial to life, every living thing shows the imprint of these shapes on its body, from the spirals of unicellular sea creatures to the whorls found in human bone. The shapes formed by flowing water can also be seen in caves, stone, river banks, clouds, and cliff sides.

The entire planet is sculpted and formed by the slipping, shifting forms of water.[121]

A body of water consists of many surfaces and shapes flowing over each other, surfaces that interact in a rhythmic fashion to create these archetypal shapes. Waves, vortices, and spirals can be found within water as well as on its surface. These shapes and movements actually increase water's capacity to carry oxygen and other substances. To demonstrate this, drink from a glass of recently poured water and from one that sat overnight. Which tastes fresher, more alive? As water sits unmoving, the oxygen and life force it carries dwindle until it is no longer a useful carrier of life. Through his research into water and its properties, author and Steiner-inspired scientist Theodor Schwenk found that there is a direct correlation between water quality and its movement.

Schwenk wondered how to help repair the damage we humans have caused in polluting, diverting, and otherwise ignorantly killing the planet's water. He asked one of his students in Germany, John Wilkes, to create sculptures that mimicked the natural flowing shapes of water, sculptures now known as flow forms. These shapes have been used to clean polluted water by increasing the vitality of the water through its natural capacity for transformation, a capacity that is vastly improved when water flows in its natural forms.[122]

Sculptural flow forms look like the inside of organs or the shape of sea coral. They mimic the natural flow of water, which can be seen in the natural shapes of all things on earth, such as shells, bones, internal organs, and the leaves of plants. To see the general shape of a flow form, drop a series of blobs of chocolate cake batter into yellow cake batter. Run a toothpick down through the center of this chain of blobs. The heart-shaped curves and spirals show you something of what a flow form looks like. Sculptural flow forms are three-dimensional forms of these shapes molded in stone or concrete over which increasingly vitalized water burbles.

Flow forms can be used in decorative elements such as the fountains set up by researcher Jennifer Greene in housing developments and parks. She says, "Wherever flow forms are, people gather."[123] The vitality of the water increases the vitality of these communities. If there is a corner of your land where you might put a fountain, consider building a flow form over which rainwater can flow or installing a pump to constantly recirculate water. See Resources for purchasing already-made flow-form fountains. Rainwater that runs over this form will be more energized when it soaks into the earth than when it fell, and birds and other animals who come to drink from your fountain will be blessed with vital, living water.

GODDESS

Chalciuhtlicue

The Aztec goddess of lakes, streams, and flowing water, Chalciuhtlicue wears a blue and white dress decorated with water lilies. Her name means "jade skirt." She presides over beauty and fertility. Images of the prickly pear and a river represent Chalciuhtlicue, for cactuses and rivers both bring hydration and beauty to the arid desert.

Chalciuhtlicue created violent floods that destroyed the fourth world when the god Quetzalcoatl drove away her lover, Tlaloc the Rain God.

Call on Chalciuhtlicue to help you build a new relationship with water or to help with fertility—in the garden, in your relationships, and in your life.

Sacred Sister: Betsy Damon

artist

Betsy Damon is best known for her work on the Living Water Project in Chengdu, China, where she brought together her love of water, community, and art to help create the first inner-city ecological park with water as its theme. The park is a fully functional water treatment plant, an environmental education center, and a refuge for plants, wildlife, and people. In the shape of a fish, the park stretches along the Fu-Nan River. The park's natural treatment system uses flow forms and other natural filters to process 200 cubic meters a day of polluted river water, producing water clean enough to drink. The system is not enough to affect the overall river quality, but is intended as an educational and inspirational feature.

In 1990, Betsy founded Keepers of the Waters, a project dedicated to combining art and science to form new ways of relating to the powerful resource of water. She visited Chengdu in the early nineties and became inspired to create the Living Water Project with local architects, artists, and concerned citizens. In 1995, she invited Chinese, Tibetan, and American artists to collaborate on a public art project designed to raise awareness about the Fu-Nan River. She returned later to meet with architects and hydrologists to look for an appropriate site for the park along this vital river. Over the two years it took to build the park, those working on the project had to face strong resistance from Chinese officials because of communist policy about public art. Much of the work and financial support for the project was garnered from locals and individual citizens; neither the Chinese nor American governments wanted to support it. At its completion, however, the Living Water Project won praise and recognition from the city's mayor and the Communist Party. It received the Top Honor Award from the Waterford Center in Washington, D.C., and a design award from the Environmental Design and Research Center.

Damon first devoted her life to water in 1985. After a day of sculpting with river mud in Castle Valley, Utah, she looked up at the night sky to discover how the whitish river blended into the sweep of the Milky Way. The water of the earth and the ancient wisdom of the stars spoke to her, and she eventually founded Keepers of the Waters. There are now similar projects in Seattle, Portland, and Duluth.

Damon wrote:

> Few people in the U.S. government or business industry can believe that a middle-aged, U.S. female did this on her own. It is clear that what I was able to accomplish need not be so unique ... Projects such as the Living Water Garden could be an integral part of many infrastructure projects. In fact, they are imperative for real and multifunctional solutions to the more and more pressing issue of the planet's water quality.[124]

When you work with water, remember Betsy's dedication to the power of water to heal communities and the environment. One person truly can make a difference.

GODDESS

Danu

The Mother of the Tuatha de Danaan, Danu's presence can be felt at all rivers and wells. When we toss a coin into a well, we call on her wisdom and prosperity magic. Danu is a goddess of abundance and can lead you with love to your true life. Her name comes from *dan*, meaning "knowledge."[125]

To honor this great mother of the Celtic lands, set up a wishing well or small pond with a fountain in your garden. Alternately, visit a local natural spring or river. Beside the pond or spring, place a stone marked with a triple spiral, which is a sign of the Goddess. Attend this spring regularly, and when you are in need of healing, simply sprinkle some of her water upon yourself.

Water Ally: Fish

Fish have long been honored cross-culturally as sacred. They are one of eight sacred symbols of the Buddha and represent Christ or the Trinity. A fish symbol on its side is known as the *Vesica piscis,* Vessel of the Fish, the sign of the yoni. The Great Mother, Kuan Yin, and Kali are all associated with this symbol. In Greek, *delphos* means both "fish" (or dolphin) and "womb." The oracle at Delphi originally belonged to the fish or dolphin goddess Themis.[126]

If you have space for an aerated pond, you may want to include fish in your garden. Include plants for shade and nutriments, a filter and pump to cleanse and oxygenate the water, and spaces such as flat stones or broken pottery for them to hide from predators. To keep your pond fresh and your fish happy, clean your pump regularly, remove excess algae and leaf litter, and use appropriate water conditioners to reduce chlorine or sludge. Consider how to include flow forms in your pond.

Keep in mind that these fish and any other life in the pond will depend on humans for survival; only create a fish pond or set up an aquarium if you will be able to care for the fish and the pond for a long time. Are you planning on relocating or are you out of town often? Can you bring them indoors when winter comes?

If you choose to have a pond or other water feature, place it in a somewhat shady place to reduce evaporation. Ask yourself what would be the smallest-sized pond you can have that will provide you with a water feature but not hoard a valuable resource. If a pond is not the best option, you may decide on other ways to bring fish energy into your garden, especially though garden art like sculptures or fish-shaped stones.

Feng shui principles teach us that fish represent wealth, so you may want to locate your pond or sculpture in the corner of your yard pertaining to money and wealth—the back left corner of your property if you stand facing your front door. However you bring fish energy into your garden, give thanks to the planet's fish for gifting us with the energies of wealth and health.

Sacred Sister: Sandra Ingerman

healer

Shaman and psychotherapist, Sandra Ingerman is best known for her teachings and writings on soul retrieval and other shamanic-based healing practices. In 2001, Ingerman applied her work to environmental issues in her book *Medicine for the Earth: How to Transform Personal and Environmental Toxins* (Three Rivers Press). This amazing book takes the reader through powerful personal transformation techniques and into the realm of transmutation or transfiguration of water. Instead of turning water into wine in the biblical sense of transmutation, the reader learns to turn polluted water into pure, light-filled, alive water.

Formerly the Educational Director of the Foundation

for Shamanic Studies, Ingerman teaches workshops on shamanism worldwide. She has an MA in Counseling Psychology from the California Institute of Integral Studies and is a licensed Marriage and Family Therapist and Professional Mental Health Counselor in the state of New Mexico.[127] Her work brings ancient methods of healing and working with spirits into a modern context. She is a very advanced practitioner, but the techniques outlined in her books and newsletters are accessible even to beginners. She is dedicated to helping all people reconnect with their deeper selves through ongoing, dedicated spiritual practice and a new approach to living in the world.

Ingerman's teachings include transmutation and transfiguration of the cells in our own bodies. She reminds her students that outer work cannot be done without dedication to inner transformation. Her work is about reconnecting with the greater organism of the planet, which will heal not only our physical pain but the epidemic hate and inequality seen in acts of terrorism, genocide, and rape. "As we allow ourselves to reconnect with the organism we are part of and evolve with it and receive and absorb nurturance from it, we reestablish coherence for the organism. Healing and evolution can occur in a harmonious fashion."[128] The "organism we are a part of" is our bodies and the planet itself. It is the people and the non-human allies that share Earth. It is the water that flows in relationship with all life. In her August, 2005, online newsletter, she writes:

As long as we see ourselves as separate from each other we forget that what we do to each other we do to ourselves. And as long as there is so much inequality there will be separation and hate. As long as there is fundamentalism around the world there will be separate camps and religious wars.

And as long as we do not honor our connection with nature, the elements will keep coming through as hurricanes, tornadoes, fires, and earthquakes to remind us how out of balance we are.

So what can we do? We can continue our spiritual work. We can find peace within. We can go inside and get very still. We keep praying and connecting to the web of life and doing our work to experience harmony within no matter what is going on around us.[129]

You can learn to transmute the water in your garden, your home, and your body, and, as Ingerman says, bring that work into the world as a sacred sister.

Transmutation

Most of the water we encounter in the modern world lacks the life and magic that pure water offers, water now found only in pristine mountain springs or burbling through human-made flow forms. True spring water is high in dissolved carbons and minerals and is infused with the nourishing energy of the mother. Tap water, on the other hand, is high in toxins like chlorine, aluminum, and fluoride. Bottled water that is not from a spring offers little more in natural hydration and clarity, for it is often purified water with added minerals—in other words, dead water with stuff mixed in.

Purchasing bottled spring water for drinking offers a partial solution to the dearth of healthy water in the average home, but would be outrageously expensive to also use for cooking and bathing. Most of us could not set up flow forms in our household plumbing. Whole house filters or filters on every faucet help remove toxins, but do nothing to rebuild the chi the water lacks. You get clean water, but it is just about energetically dead. This solution can also be too expensive for many.

There is, however, a powerful and fully accessible way to get natural energized water in your home, called transmutation. Sandra Ingerman teaches the process of transmutation in her classes in Santa Fe, New Mexico, and in her book *Medicine for the Earth.* Stated simply, transmutation involves merging with the divine and inviting water, or any other energy, to do the same. When we reconnect with our true divine self, we step back into the pure, nourishing energy of Goddess essence. For this you must release the boundaries you have believed true: namely, that you are separate from what is "outside" you and that you are separate from the divine. The universality of water and its constantly flowing relationships illustrate most clearly that these perceptions are false.

Transmutation is a mindfulness practice in itself. To begin, pour a glass or fill a bowl with water. Take a sip of the water to taste it before your meditation. Sit where you will not be disturbed, and come into a present, grounded state. Now bring to your mind a picture of the Creator. For me, this image is sometimes a rainbow-colored flame, other times it is more a feeling than an image, a sense of vastness and creative power. Sometimes

I see Her as a woman. Picture and feel this symbol strongly, then impose it over the image of yourself. Become this image. You are the Creator; your distinct energy that you know of as yourself has now merged with the Infinite Creator. Feel your energy expand into the infinite universe. Sit with this feeling and image until it is very clear and strong. You may hear something as well, like a beautiful song.

Now bring your attention to the water in your cup. Feel it as the Creator as well. It is part of the infinite divine universe. Become aware of its consciousness. Invite it to reflect the same glory with which you have merged, to vibrate in union with the Creator. Invite the water to live in its purest essence.

Sitting in union with the Creator can feel infinitely beautiful and terribly overwhelming. Breathe steadily and let yourself sink into the union you have forgotten. Vibrate here as long as you like. Feel your communion with the universe and the glass of water. When you are ready, open your eyes. Taste the water.

Ingerman's studies show how physical toxins and pollutants can be cleared via transmutation. After reading her book, I tried the practice on a half gallon of tap water, generally considered not toxic. I did not test the contents of the water before and after, as Ingerman has done repeatedly, but the taste of the water after the transmutation blew me away. It tasted of fresh mountain snow or a spring gurgling up from the heart of the earth—certainly the best water I have ever tasted.

Practice transmutation regularly to improve your ability to release into the divine, and you will easily transmute all water you come in contact with: drinking water, cooking water, bath water. You can also perform this exercise with other substances, emotions, or situations, for everything is energy. This practice raises the energy of a substance or situation into union with the creator. Through this work, applied with pure intent, anything can become one with its divine purpose.

Practice transmutation in the garden to raise the energy of your plants, pond or fountain, and land. Transmute the water in the watering can. Charge the hose that delivers water to the earth. Charge and transmute bird seed and suet you have put out for your feathered friends. Not only will your garden be a magical place of healing and power, your whole life will transform to one of light, health, and divine energy.

GODDESS

Anahita

The Persian Goddess of water and fertility, Anahita embodies fertility and the sweet blessing of rain. Dressed in gold and otter skins, she rides a chariot driven by four white horses: hail, wind, rain, and clouds. To ensure sweet rains upon your garden, or to enhance your fertility, light green candles and call on Anahita. Make love beneath the stars in her name.

Water Ally: Turtle

Turtle teaches us about longevity and authenticity. Her shell is both her spine and her home. She can feel vibrations in water through her skin and shell, an intelligence you can learn from as you develop your own "extra"-sensory perception. Call on Turtle to teach you about paying attention.

Like many other water allies, the turtle teaches us about transitioning from earth to water. Turtles lay their eggs on land, though they may spend the rest of their lives in water. Sea turtles often gather from all over the ocean to lay their eggs in large groups on one or two special beaches. They coordinate this gathering by the moon and tides. When the baby turtles hatch, usually all at once, they crawl to water by the hundreds. Such large numbers ensure their safety from predators. Turtle can teach us about the value of community and cooperation as well as the importance of right timing.

First Nations Peoples call planet Earth *Turtle Island,* for it is told in many stories how a great turtle carries the Earth on her solid back. Turtle can teach us about being Earth stewards and protecting our piece of the Earth in any way we can, as turtle did for the First Peoples.

If you choose to bring a turtle into your home, research its origins first. Some turtles are endangered or threatened, and not all pet stores or dealers act with ecological responsibility. Also take time to learn about turtle care, and consider if a turtle is the right ally for your yard or home. Turtles live a long time; carefully consider if you can care for this companion for the next forty years or more. Never take any animal into your home that you cannot care for indefinitely.

If you don't have the space or inclination for a turtle pond in your garden, bring turtle energy into your space with turtle and tortoise statues or decorate mosaic stepping stones with turtle imagery.

WATER ALLY: FROG

Frogs teach us about clean but appropriate boundaries. A useful metaphor for healthy physical and psychological boundaries is the semi-permeable membrane, like cell walls and the amphibious skin of the frog. Semi-permeable membranes allow for the ebb and flow of natural living. Balanced frog energy means you can cry or sweat to cleanse your body and mind, and you take in enough clean water to wash your cells with the flow of life.

Sacred to Venus and Hecate, also called Hekat or Hekt, the frog is an Egyptian symbol of the fetus. A symbol of nine frogs was used as a fertility charm in Babylon. The frog also represents the yoni, cave to the great womb.[130] Because of its amphibious nature,

Frog can help us travel from the world of air (the mind) to water (the heart or dreams) or into the Underworld. Frog hibernates in colder regions by burrowing into mud, where she goes dormant for the winter, emerging in spring as renewed as Persephone.

Frogs are well adapted to many damp, non-saline environments, such as wetlands, rotting logs, humid forests, and ponds and streams. However, their evolution over millions of years did not include until very recently such pollutants as chemical pesticides and fertilizers. The introduction of these poisons by humans, plus riparian habitat destruction from agriculture, recreation, and urbanization, have led to the epidemic decline of frog populations worldwide. The destruction of the ozone layer may also contribute to declining frog populations due to increased UV radiation.

For four hundred million years, frogs have filled an important ecological niche, eating insects and fish, and feeding birds, mammals, and larger fish. By destroying their habitats, we invite overpopulation of insects and the destruction of frog predators. You can help support frog populations by providing cool, aerated pond space in your garden. Use no chemical fertilizers or pesticides on your lawn or garden. Dispose of oil, antifreeze, and other household chemicals responsibly, through local gas stations or toxic waste receptacles. If you live near a wetland or other riparian zone, participate in local and state actions to restore and protect these extremely important and endangered habitats. When you journey in forests and near ponds, tread lightly. Never drive a vehicle through streams or ponds, and take care when entering water with a boat.

Watering the Garden

"Water will always attempt to form an organic whole by joining what is divided and uniting it in circulation. It is not possible to speak of the beginning or end of a circulatory system; everything is inwardly connected and reciprocally related. Water is essentially the element of circulatory systems."

Theodor Schwenk[131]

Water is the blood of Earth, from the oceans to the skies to the vascular system of every plant and animal. Water connects all. Remember this and all the aspects of water you have just read when thinking about water in the garden. When working with any energy, including water, you deal with input, storage, and output. In the case of watering the garden, input sources include direct rain, plumbing, and sometimes irrigation channels. Storage can be in the soil or in a water catchment system like a rain barrel. Output includes the act of watering your beds and lawn.

All of the parts of water usage can be made more efficient by reducing waste or conserving the water you use by using it most wisely. To reduce waste, avoid excess evaporation by mulching, planting seedlings close together in fertile soil, and applying water only as needed.

The exact amount of water a plant needs depends on what climate it is adapted to; plants from arid regions need less water than fruits developed in humid areas. Most plants extract water from the air space in the soil around their roots, so matching the soil needs of each plant will help ensure efficient water supply.

Even if you live in a moist climate with plenty of rainfall, conserve water wherever possible. By being mindful of your water use in the garden, you leave water for the natural communities around you—and for the future. Water-wise gardening begins by observing the land and planting wisely. Group plants with similar water needs, providing plant communities with appropriate soil type, wind, and sun exposure. Observe sun, wind, and shade areas of your land throughout the year to get an idea of the best location for these groupings, and ask the nature spirits or the land itself where to put your plants. Choose plant varieties suited to your climate's rainfall, heat, soil type, and growing season.

Drip irrigation is the most efficient way to get water to your plants, especially in climates that tend toward dryness. Drip irrigation reduces water loss due to evaporation, is easy and inexpensive to build, is very flexible, and offers an opportunity to water deeply at plants' roots. Drip irrigation decreases the amount of water lost to evaporation by 50 to 70 percent over spraying with a sprinkler, increasing efficiency and decreasing waste. You can tailor a drip irrigation system to provide exactly the right amount of water to a variety of areas. Since the system is so efficient, you can often water only a few times a week for an hour at a time. Such a system not only gets more water deeper in the soil, helping plants develop deep, strong root systems, it lets water know that it is valued and tells it exactly where you want its energy to go. Remember that water carries not only nutrients and electrons, but energy and intentions. The plants will carry these focused intentions in their very structure.

For information on setting up your own drip irrigation system, see Water Resources. Your cooperative extension office will likely offer free fact sheets on drip irrigation as well. A good local nursery will offer classes on drip irrigation, and supplies for building your own can be purchased at local hardware stores or those same good nurseries. It only takes an afternoon or two of measuring, cutting, and putting together a system that will serve your garden for years, and which costs much less than an overhead sprinkler system.

For a smaller garden, using a bucket and a small container to water directly at plant's roots can reduce water waste. Transmute the water in the bucket before you water as a daily meditation and spiritual garden practice.

Water early in the morning before the sun gets too hot. Never water in the heat of the day. You will lose too much to evaporation and can even cook your veggies or seeds. In dry climates you can also water in the evening, but in a humid climate this can invite mildew growth as water sits on leaves and at the root line for a long time in cool night air. Plants open their stomata at night and exhale, so they are increasing the relative humidity around them, further increasing the wetness that can invite mildew and fungus growth.

Water can also be conserved by using the best storage unit for your climate and garden. The best place to store garden water is in soil, which can hold large amounts of water in the spaces between soil particles, and by hydrating organic matter like peat moss; fertile soil can hold more water and support more plants per square inch. You may not usually think of the soil itself as a storage unit, but utilizing the properties of soil and other ground covers to conserve water respects the nature of water and soil. Water wants to flow, to interact with the land and the air. It wants to move in natural, curving spaces. By maximizing the amount of water your soil will hold in proportion to your plants' needs, you reduce waste and create a more alive garden.

Mulching around plants helps to conserve moisture, moderate soil temperature, and discourage weeds. Mulch is any matter, preferably organic, that covers the soil. Ask your garden what kind of mulch is appropriate for your climate. Mulch need not be expensive; decayed hay, fallen leaves, and grass clippings all work well. Your city may even provide free mulch to residents; call the forestry division or check your city's website for details. My city delivers a truckload of wood-chip mulch for free simply to be rid of it; I love having the monster pile in my driveway, waiting to be distributed throughout my yard and garden. Talk about abundance!

The soil can also be contoured to catch surface and rainwater using a swale, a shallow trench following the contour of the land and lined on the downhill side with a small berm. Over time, water infiltrates the swale and develops a miniature aquifer of stored water that deep-rooted plants can tap into. For detailed information on building swales in your garden, see Toby Hemenway's *Gaia's Garden.*

Water can also be stored in non-soil catchment systems such as rain barrels. Attaching several rain barrels to your house and other buildings catches rain from the roof, rather than sending it all into expensive and wasteful sewage treatment systems. Ideally, rain barrels and other storage units are made not of plastic, which will be with us forever and leaches poisons into the water, but of wood or another natural substance. Use the water in your barrels frequently to allow the water to keep moving. Water that sits too long becomes dead water and loses its vitality. Storing water for too long also keeps it from other beings who need it; aquifers, rivers, wildlife, and wild lands are as equally deserving of rainwater as we are.

There are other ways to use water efficiently, either instead of or along with a rain barrel. Boost water use by sharing space in a community garden. Water your lawn as little as possible, or plant drought-tolerant plants and ground-cover instead of grass. Mulch around your plants, and plant native or naturalized species. Water infrequently and deeply. Place your garden where it will receive as much rain and runoff as possible without actively diverting natural flow by observing how water moves, or would move, through your property. Plant in low-lying areas or along real or imaginary river beds by following the contours of the land.

Watering the garden efficiently benefits from a few techniques like mulching and drip irrigation, but also from approaching water as the magical, sentient being it is.

Water Magic in the Garden

We influence everything we come in contact with; as you interact with water throughout your day, become conscious of this power. In the garden, set up systems that honor the nature of water and the powers of transformation that can occur through conscious relationship. The energy of water can be raised and the water cleansed as it flows naturally through your garden, across your patio, and around your home. Take inspiration from your sacred sisters and use art, science, and spiritual practice to craft a water-charging center in your back yard or community garden space.

A simple way to charge water as it flows through your yard is to create a series of ceramic or stone containers over which the water flows. Each container can have a word or symbol carved into it like *love, peace, roots,* or *inspire*. Sculpt the bowls yourself or purchase containers from a garden center and fill with engraved stones, available at many garden-themed gift stores. Take time every now and then to sit with the bowls and the stones, and send the intentions of your chosen words into the medium. The water will be charged with these intentions and bring power into the earth.

You might place large shells, with permission from the previous inhabitants, throughout your garden as well. Shells are natural flow forms, and as rain or hose water runs over and through these shells, the water will be charged with a greater capacity to hold light and energy.

Consider ways to charge the water you use for irrigation as well. If you utilize a drip line, you might decorate the plastic tubing, using nontoxic paints, with words or symbols of intention. As the water flows through this oblong container, it will become infused with the energies and intentions you have offered. Your plants and the soil allies will also benefit.

To water potted plants or isolated areas of the garden, fill a bucket with water and take a moment to transmute the water before pouring it onto the earth. Notice how this practice changes your consciousness of your relationship with the water, the land, and the plants.

When repairing or putting in a new patio or driveway, sculpt flow forms into the sides of the concrete. Divert water from low areas with meandering or spiral-shaped channels. In nature, water always moves in flow forms, not straight lines. Mimic natural shapes to enliven water as it flows through your yard, nourishing the land.

You might also turn areas that have trouble draining into dry river beds; when it rains, the water will have a natural path to follow instead of becoming stuck. To build a riverbed, follow the contour of your land the way water would naturally flow. Clear the area of weeds, and cover it with landscape fabric. Place the largest stones in the middle of the riverbed and medium-sized ones along its banks. On the outside of any curve, form a little sandy or pebbled beach. Fill in the spaces with any smaller or mid-sized stones or pebbles that you like, mimicking the way a river distributes stones and sand along its flow. If you live in a wetter climate, you might plant ferns and other moisture-loving plants along the banks of your sometimes-river. A river bed in a dry climate can be a home to irises, grasses, and violets.

These are but a few ways to revitalize water on your land and in your garden. Bringing new consciousness about water beyond the garden is equally crucial. Introduce flow forms and transmutation to your community through ritual or political action. Team up with local stream recovery efforts and include sculptural elements intended to revitalize and educate. Give talks at local schools and community centers on the nature of water, and include interactive play with flow forms (an easy and dramatic demonstration can be set up by dropping food coloring into a glass). Ask yourself how you can be an agent for forming a new ethic based on the spiritual and life-giving power of water.

Sacred Sister: Starhawk

activist

Starhawk is best known as a Witch and activist, working from a spiritually based perspective on political and environmental issues. Her book *The Spiral Dance: A Rebirth of the Ancient Religion of the Great Goddess,* originally published in 1979, has been foundational for many discovering neo-paganism and contemporary Witchcraft. She co-founded Reclaiming, a tradition of the Craft that incorporates activism into their work, including many actions relating to water as a right for all life. Her novel *The Fifth Sacred Thing* won the Lambda Award for best Gay and Lesbian Science Fiction in 1994—and inspired me to become a healer. One of her most recent books, *Webs of Power: Notes from the Global Uprising,* won a 2003 Nautilus Award in the social change category. She recently completed a film on the life of archaeologist Marija Gimbutas, who made major discoveries about Goddess cultures of Old Europe.

Together with Penny Livingston-Stark and Erik Ohlsen, Starhawk co-teaches Earth Activist Trainings (EAT), intensive trainings that combine political activism, permaculture design, and earth-based spirituality. Her intention through these trainings and her own work is to restore the balance on the planet. She is also an organic gardener practicing permaculture, a design system that seeks to create sustainable habitats by following nature's patterns. She writes in *The Earth Path: Grounding Your Spirit in the Rhythms of Nature:*

> Some years ago, when a group of us had just acquired land in the coastal hills of northern California, I was meditating in our garden. I was questioning my own driving need to garden in an environment that was already beautiful and needed no improvement. The garden said to me, "Grow food. I want you to grow food—because if you eat the food that comes from this land, you will be the land." ... Even if we grow only a small amount, growing and eating food from our place will establish a relationship with it. If nothing else, grow a few herbs or some mint in a windowsill, and use them in rituals and for tea.[132]

Starhawk lives and teaches that all of life is connected. We are a part of Earth, of the Goddess: the dance of birth, growth, death, and regeneration. Our actions make a difference, from marching against non-sustainable big business and irresponsible politicians to growing and buying local organic food. She reminds us that our sacred work as healers, Witches, women, and earth activists must come from an ongoing and strong connection with the earth, which we develop and strengthen by regularly spending time in nature, including wilderness and the garden.

Water Magic: Manifesting Your Dreams

We have toured the garden through the four sacred elements of earth, air, fire, and water. You have prepared the soil, planted seeds, and given thanks and respect for the sun and water. You have dreamed of ways to bring the powerful gift of the garden to others through community while healing the earth by going organic. Goddesses and sacred sisters from around the world have walked with you along a path of discovery, returning you to your deepest potential and opening doors of new life. Now it is time to call on the powers of water, of dreaming and connection and movement, to craft yourself as a steward of the sacred land through the garden and beyond.

I hope you see how the garden truly can make a difference in healing the sacred land. The chemicals you use or do not use make a difference to the beings of the soil, water, and air. Organic soil traps greenhouse gases. Water can be cleansed through meditation, intention, and the shape it follows as it flows. Gardening with and for others changes the face of the neighborhood and assures a better life for children. Returning the land to native growth renews life and vitality, making it whole again.

All of these actions speak of a new ethic of the land itself. They come about from relationship with Earth, the planets, and the plants and animals and people with whom we live. They make up the solid, long arm of the tree of change. They weave a Celtic knot of compassion and wholeness that cannot be broken. You are a part of that weave, a branch on that tree. You have a part in healing the land. What will your part be?

It is not enough to read about the garden. Once you encounter the power of the land to heal and make whole, you want to share this truth. You want to give back to the planet. Understanding the interdependence of ecology, spirituality, and everyday action, you want to protect the land you love so deeply, the allies and wild ones and green growing beings. Listen to the urge bursting in your heart to take action and live passionately in the garden of the Goddess.

The Shuar Indians of Ecuador believe that we dream the world, that we create the world with our dreams. If we want to change the world, we have to change the dream. First, you must know what you are dreaming. Then you must learn to dream consciously, to change your dream to create the world in which you wish to live.

When you go to bed tonight, ask the devas to send you a dream. Keep a dream journal for several nights, keeping track of recurring images or themes. Look for synchronicities in waking life as well: animal allies, stories you hear on the news, images in the clouds, or random phone calls from an old friend. Pay attention to your body, to any symptoms you feel; this is your subconscious mind talking to you in metaphor.

Go back and read the journals you have kept as you read this book. Notice any themes, any questions or yearnings that arose for you. Let all these images and experiences float through your mind. Paint them, sing them, tell them to the trees. When an idea of your own action begins to form, write about it in your garden journal.

Not only will you discover what you wish to dream, but parts of you that inhibit your dream may surface. These are the voices, call them nightmares, that say you are too small, stupid, busy, or too whatever to craft a dream world. Listen to these voices, for they are powerful—and then invite them to leave. Thank them for their wisdom, and then let them go. You no longer need them. Now you need the voice of your inner Goddess. It is She who will craft a sacred world.

To see your passion and your dreams more clearly, ask yourself the following questions:

- What is your work as a sacred sister?
- What change do you wish to see that you might bring to the world through the garden?
- Which garden allies spoke most clearly to you?
- Which goddesses resonated deep in your heart?
- What did you learn from your meditations?
- What did you discover in the ocean with Yemaya? In the garden with Eve?
- You have seen that one woman living her dream can make a big difference. What vision do you wish to dream into reality?
- What feelings arise in your body as you contemplate manifesting your own dreams, passions, and world-sweeping changes?

Women have been taught to fear our power and to fear change. Historically—and in many cases this is still true—women who stood up for their families, the land, or themselves were burned, raped, murdered, and shamed. Those of us who live in safe environments still carry that fear in our bones. We must let that fear go. The life and health of the Mother Earth depends on our reclaiming our power as women to heal, to shake up the status quo, and to breed compassion.

Call on the allies, plants, goddesses, and fellow sisters to give you strength and guidance along your path. Join other women of power in dreaming the world anew. As a group of stewards dedicated to sacred work with the land, we can make a difference. Whether you are a mover and a shaker on the protest lines or one who stands up for the value of soil bacteria, or both, you are a part of a large and powerful movement of healing with the sacred land.

I invite you to share your story with others. Visit www.IntuitiveGardening.net to share your own dreams and projects of power. Through this website, powerful gardeners from throughout the world gather in a great circle of love for the earth, the garden, and each other.

Together, we reclaim our heritage as women of the Earth. Let us gather and call in a new era of old wisdom and new understanding. We are the stewards of the sacred land, walking the garden paths and sharing our harvest with all the Earth. Blessed be!

Water Resources

Drip Irrigation

A good basic website on drip irrigation can be found at www.irrigationtutorials.com/dripguide.htm, provided by Jess Stryker, landscape architect. His site is comprehensive and easy to understand.

Also see:

DripWorks, Inc.
190 Sanhedrin Circle
Willits, CA 95490
(707) 459-6323 (design and tech support)
(800) 522-3747 (to order supplies or request a catalogue)
www.dripworksusa.com

Flow Forms

Sensitive Chaos: The Creation of Flowing Forms in Water and Air by Theodor Schwenk (Rudolph Steiner Press, 1990)

A fantastic exploration of the nature of water and air and how vital water is the key to life. Includes many illustrations and photographs. Out of print but available through interlibrary loan.

To purchase flow-form fountains, visit Flowforms America at http://www.flowformsamerica.com (877) 642-2810, or Designs for Life at www.flowforms.com (in New Zealand).

For pictures of flow form fountains, see the National Water Center's website, www.nationalwatercenter.org/ff__pictures.htm. Also see A. John Wilkes' book *Flowforms: The Rhythmic Power of Water* (Floris Books, 2003).

See Keepers of the Water's website. This site shows a collection of water parks intended for revitalization. They can help you set up a local project as well.

They can be contacted at:

Keepers of the Water
P. O. Box 80637
Portland, OR 97280
www.keepersofthewater.org

The Water Research Institute of Blue Hill studies flow forms and other ways of working with vital water. They offer an educational program for schools.

The Water Research Institute of Blue Hill
POB 930, Route 177
Redwing Lane
Blue Hill, Maine 04614
(207) 374-2384
Fax (207) 374-2383
www.waterresearch.org

Transmutation

See Sandra Ingerman's website, which includes links to class schedules, information on her books, and a monthly online newsletter.

She can also be contacted at:

Sandra Ingerman
P.O. Box 4757
Santa Fe, NM 87502
www.shamanicvisions.com/ingerman.html

Earth Activist Trainings

"Earth Activist Training blends a full permaculture certification course with Earth-based spirituality, practical political effectiveness, and nature awareness. Learn how to transform land, communities, political systems, and yourself. Discover solutions, renew personal energy, and find hope for our world." From their website, www.earthactivisttraining.org/.

Earth Activist Training
P. O. Box 251
Sierraville, CA 96126
info@earthactivisttraining.org

in the UK:

Earth Activist Training UK
c/o 3 Yew Tree Cottages
Pitt Court
North Nibley
Gloucester Gl11 6EB
eat2006@riseup.net

Notes

Notes

Endnotes

1 Walker, *The Woman's Encyclopedia of Myths and Secrets,* 218.

2 Stewart, *The Earth Moved,* 103.

3 Ibid., 151.

4 Starhawk, *The Earth Path,* 163.

5 Wyant, "Gardening Views You Can Use," 68.

6 Muten, *Goddesses of World Myth and Magic,* 45.

7 See The Pachamama Alliance at pachamama.org/.

8 Sams and Carson, 209.

9 Ibid., 210.

10 Murray, 105–106.

11 Rebecca Dye, personal email conversation, 23 February 2005.

12 Jane Resture, "Maori Mythology: Polynesia, The Origin of Mankind," www.janeresture.com/polynesia__myths/new zealand.htm (accessed 13 August 2006).

13 Burleigh Muten, *Goddesses of World Myth and Magic* (Cambridge, MA: Barefoot Books, 2003), 14.

14 Conway, *Magick of the Gods and Goddesses,* 394–395.

15 Hafiz, "Your Seed Pouch," *The Gift,* 41.

16 Jeavons, *How to Grow More Vegetables,* 46.

17 Lauren Artress, The Labyrinth Society, www.labyrinthsociety.org/ (accessed 2 November 2004).

18 Sue Monk Kidd, *Dance of the Dissident Daughter* (New York: Harper SanFrancisco, 1996), 115.

19 Walker, 786.

20 Hemenway, *Gaia's Garden,* 5.

21 Heaton, 36–37.

22 Stewart, *The Earth Moved,* 122.

23 Lisbeth Grinder-Pedersen, Salka E. Rusmussen, Susanne Bügel, Lars V. Jørgensen, Lars O. Dragsted, Vagn Gundersen, and Brittmarie Sandström, "Effect of Diets Based on Foods from Conventional Versus Organic Production on Intake and Excretion of Flavonoids and Markers of Antioxidative Defense in Humans," *Journal of Agriculture and Food Chemistry,* 51:19 (2003),5671–5676.

24 Cleeton, "Organic Foods in Relation to Nutrition and Health Key Facts," 11 July 2004. This factsheet is a summary of an article published in Coronary and

Diabetic Care in the UK 2004 by the Association of Primary Care Groups and Trusts (UK). www.organicconsumers.org/organic/organic__health__062903.cfm (accessed 8 December 2005).

25 Pesticide Action Network, "Pesticide Residues from Non-Organic Foods Building Up in Our Bodies," 11 May 2004, www.organicconsumers.org/foodsafety/residues052404.cfm (accessed 8 December 2005).

26 Kristen S. Schafer, Margaret Reeves, Skip Spitzer, and Susan Kegley, "Chemical Trespass: Pesticides in Our Bodies and Corporate Accountability," *Pesticide Action Network North America* (May 2004), 6.

27 Pesticide Action Network, "Pesticide Residues from Non-Organic Foods Building Up in Our Bodies," 11 May 2004, www.organicconsumers.org/foodsafety/residues052404.cfm (accessed 8 December 2005).

28 E. Tielmans, et al., "Pesticide Exposure and Decreased Fertilization Rates In Vitro," *Lancet*, 484–5.

29 Sandra Steingraber, *Having Faith: An Ecologist's Journey to Motherhood* (Cambridge: Perseus Books Group, 2001), 253.

30 E. Tielmans, et al., "Pesticide Exposure and Decreased Fertilization Rates In Vitro," *Lancet*, 484–5.

31 Assadourian, "Cultivating the Butterfly Effect," *World Watch Magazine*, 34.

32 Leiss and Savitz, "Home Pesticide Use and Childhood Cancer," 249–252.

33 Worldwatch Institute, "Globetrotting Food Will Travel Farther Than Ever This Thanksgiving," press release, 21 November 2002 (accessed 25 March 2005 at www.worldwatch.org/press/news/2002/11/21/).

34 Sullivan, "Organic Gardens Help Fight Global Warming," *Organic Gardening*, Jan/Feb 2004, 51 (accessed 27 January 2007 at www.organicgardening.com/feature/0,7518,s1-4-63-1321,00.html).

35 Bill McKibben, *Maybe One: A Case for Smaller Families* (New York: Plume Books, 1999), 104.

36 Halweil, "Home Grown: The Case for Local Food in a Global Market," *Worldwatch Paper* 163, November 2002.

37 Pollan, *The Omnivore's Dilemma*, 214.

38 Ausubel, *Restoring the Earth*, 130.

39 Moskin, "Women Find Their Place in the Field," *The New York Times*, 1 June 2005 (accessed online 1 June 2005 at www.nytimes.com).

40 Hoffman, *The New Holistic Herbal*, 34.

41 Small Wright, *Co-Creative Science*, 21.

42 *Spirit in the Smokies*, "Dorothy MacLean: A Spirit in the Smokies Interview," 25 May 1999 (accessed 10 June 2005 at www.spiritinthesmokies.com/interviews/dorothym.html).

43 Ibid.

44 Muten, 22.

45 *The Old Farmer's Almanac* (Dublin, NH: Yankee Publishing, 2006). www.almanac.com.

46 Jose Arguelles, *The Mayan Factor: Path Beyond Technology* (Santa Fe: Bear & Co., 1996).

47 Cunningham, *Cunningham's Encyclopedia of Magical Herbs*, 271.

48 Northup, 104, 107.

49 Cunningham, *Cunningham's Encyclopedia of Magical Herbs*, 272.

50 Ibid.

51 Ibid.

52 Chogyam Trungpa, *Shambhala: The Sacred Path of the Warrior* (Boston: Shambhala, 1984), 28.

53 Cunningham, 273.

54 Ibid.

55 Ibid.

56 "Correspondences of Neptune," Alchemy Works (accessed 21 March 2005 at www.alchemy-works.com/planets__neptune.html).

57 "Correspondences of Pluto," Alchemy Works (accessed 22 March 2005 at www.alchemy-works.com/planets__pluto.html).

58 *Florida Gardener.com*, "Cornflowers, Bachelor's Buttons, Basket Flowers, or the Old-Fashioned Blue Bottle" (accessed 15 August 2006 at www.floridagardener.com/misc/Cornflowers.htm).

59 Donna Carey and MichelAngelo, "Sedna: The Mysteries, Miracle, and Infinite Capacity of Water Remembering the Past and Future of Oriental Medicine," *Oriental Medicine Journal*, Winter 2006, 6–17.

60 Ellie Crystal, "Seshat, The Scribe," Crystalinks (accessed 27 January 2007 at www.crystalinks.com/seshat.html).

61 Carr-Gomm, *The Druid Animal Oracle*, 111.

62 Walker, 408.

63 Miller's Honey Company, "How Honey Is Made" (accessed 12 February 2007 at www.millershoney.com/making/htm).

64 John E. Losey and Mace Vaughn, "The Economic Value of Ecological Services Provided by Insects," *BioScience* (vol. 56, no. 4, April 2006), 315, and Peter G.Keran and Truman P. Phillips, "The Economic Impacts of Pollinator Declines: An Approach to Assessing the Consequences," *Conservation Ecology* (vol. 5, no. 1, June 2001; accessed 28 January 2007 at www.minfully.org/Farm/Pollinator-Declines.htm).

65 Roger A. Morse and Nicholas W. Calderone, "The Value of Honey Bees as Pollinators of U.S. Crops in 2000," *Bee Culture Magazine*, March 2000.

66 Brenda Adderly, "The Latest Buzz on Products of the Hive," *Better Nutrition* (vol. 61, issue 6, August 1999), 43.

67 *Honey: A Reference Guide to Nature's Sweetener* (Longmont, CO: National Honey Board, 2005).

68 Gladstar, *Family Herbal*, 64.

69 Curott, *Witchcrafting*, 313.

70 Walker, 101.

71 Sams and Carson, *Medicine Cards*, and Carr-Gomm, *The Druid Animal Oracle*.

72 Emmanuel Kojorkwarteng, "Facts and Amazing Things

About Bats," *Prêmio de Reportage Sobre Biodiversidade* (accessed 28 January 2007 at www.biodiversityreporting.org).

73 Ackerman, 17.

74 Bat Conservation International (accessed 18 August 2006 at www.batcon.org/home/default.asp).

75 "Dragonfly," *Wikipedia* (accessed 28 January 2007 at www.en.wikipedia.org/wiki/Dragonfly).

76 Sams and Carson, 145.

77 Jose Hobday, lecture at University of Creation Spirituality 30 January 2004.

78 Quoted in *Denver's Carriage Lots,* a brochure produced by the National Park Service, Highland United Neighbors, Inc., and Denver Urban Gardens. To order, call DUG at (303) 292-9900.

79 Hackman and Wagner, "The senior gardening and nutrition project," *Journal of Nutrition Education*, 262–270.

80 Assadourian, "Cultivating the Butterfly Effect," *World Watch Magazine*, 31.

81 Been, "The Effect of Community Gardens on Neighboring Property Values," NYU Law and Economics Research Paper No. 06-09 (accessed 20 September 2006 at Social Science Research Network, ssrn.com/abstract=889113).

82 Quoted in *Denver's Carriage Lots,* a brochure produced by the National Park Service, Highland United Neighbors, Inc., and Denver Urban Gardens. To order, call DUG at (303) 292-9900.

83 Hemenway, xvi.

84 All quotes and facts from a personal interview with Judy Elliott, conducted 23 May 2005.

85 Bill Arnett, "The Sun" (accessed 6 February 2006 at www.nineplanets.org/sol.html).

86 Shannon Lee, et al., "Solar Folklore," Stanford Solar Center website (accessed 6 February 2006 at solar-center.stanford.edu/folklore.html.

87 Larry Edwards, lecture at Creation Spirituality University 1 February 2004.

88 Quoted in Ausubel, 101.

89 Cunningham, *Cunningham's Encyclopedia of Crystal, Gem, and Metal Magic*, 216.

90 Cunningham, *Cunningham's Encyclopedia of Magical Herbs*, 274–5.

91 Walker, 288.

92 Clark, "Social Lives of Rattlesnakes," *Natural History*, 37–42.

93 Conway, 367.

94 Cunningham, *Cunningham's Encyclopedia of Magical Herbs*, 218–219.

95 Hoffman, 229.

96 Ibid.

97 Barrette, "Greenwitch," *Circle Network News* (accessed 4 February 2007 at PenUltimate Productions, www.worthlink.net/~ysabet/spirit/paganpoe-1996.html).

98 *Herbal Voices*, "Glad for the Wild Garden" (accessed 10 June 2005 at www.awakenedwoman.com/rosemary__gladstar.htm).

99 Gladstar and Hirsch, *Planting the Future*, 13–16.

100 "Goga," Ra-Hoor-Khuit network (accessed 6 August 2006 at www.rahoorkhuit.net).

101 Franklin, *Midsummer*, 31.

102 Franklin, *Lammas*, 86.

103 Judith Stone, "Force of Nature," *O, the Oprah Magazine* (June 2005), 72.

104 *BBC News*, "Profile: Wangari Maathai," 8 October 2004 (accessed 25 July 2005 at news.bbc.co.uk/1/hi/world/africa/3726084.stm).

105 Stone, 72.

106 Ibid., 72.

107 Mia MacDonald and Danielle Nierenberg, "Don't Get Mad, Get Elected: A Conversation with Kenyan Activist Wangari Maathai," *World Watch* (May/June 2004), 27.

108 Anna Bond, "Enlivening Water," *Aubrey News: Aubrey's Herbals* (Winter/Spring 1998), 1. (accessed 14 July 2004 at www.organicanews.com/news/article.cfm?story__id=19).

109 Marks, *The Holy Order of Water*, 25.

110 Conway, 259.

111 Curott, 83.

112 Postel and Richter, *Rivers for Life*, 20–25.

113 Emoto, *The Hidden Messages in Water*, 5.

114 Ibid., 8.

115 Ibid., 58.

116 Ausubel, *Restoring the Earth*, 213.

117 Postel and Richter, 203.

118 Marks, 42.

119 Summers, "How Trees Get High," *Natural History*, 35.

120 Gail Johnson, "Deer Deterrents," *Gardening How-To* (September/ October 2006), 14.

121 Schwenk, *Sensitive Chaos*, 13.

122 Ausubel, *Restoring the Earth*, 217–218.

123 Ibid., 222.

124 Damon and Mavor, "The Living Water Garden," *Whole Earth* (Spring 2000, (100), 22.

125 Hrana Janto, "Danu" (accessed 9 February 2007 at www.hranajanto.com/danu.html).

126 Walker, 313.

127 *Medicine for the Earth: Sandra Ingerman's Homepage*, "About Sandra, Her Books and Tapes" (access at www.shamanicvisions.com/ingerman__folder/04books.html).

128 Sandra Ingerman, "Transmutation News July 2005," *Medicine for the Earth: Sandra Ingerman's Homepage* (accessed 22 September 2005 at www.shamanicvisions.com/ingerman__folder/05july.html).

129 Sandra Ingerman, "Transmutation News August 2005," *Medicine for the Earth: Sandra Ingerman's Homepage* (accessed 22 September 2005 at www.shamanicvisions.com/ingerman__folder/05august.html).

130 Walker, 326.

131 Schwenk, 13.

132 Starhawk, *The Earth Path*, 177–118.

APPENDIX

Organic Gardening Associations in the U.S. and Canada

This is an incomplete list; check with your favorite local garden store or extension office for more organizations near you. These are alphabetical by name.

Arlington Organic Garden Club
P. O. Box 173954
Arlington, TX 76003-3954
board@aogc.org
(972) 642-6346
www.aogc.org

Common Ground Organic Garden Supply and Education Center
559 College Avenue
Palo Alto, CA 94306
manager@commongroundinpaloalto.org
www.commongroundinpaloalto.org

The Community School Gardens and CSA
1164 Bunker Hill Rd.
Tamworth, NH 03883
garden@communityschoolnh.org
(603) 323-7000
www.communityschoolnh.org

Food For Everyone Foundation
848 Woodruff Way
Salt Lake City, Utah 84108
jim@foodforeveryone.org
(801) 583-4449
www.foodforeveryone.org

Front Range Organic Gardeners (FROG)
2160 South Sherman St.
Denver, CO 80210

Idaho Falls Community Garden Association
P.O. Box 2700
Idaho Falls, ID 83403
letsgrow@srv.net
(208) 522-3244
www.srv.net/~klack/com__gard.htm

Indiana Organic Gardeners Association
5360 East 161st St.
Noblesville, IN 46060-6916
mkraft2@earthlink.net
(317) 773-5361
www.gardeningnaturally.org

Island Mountain Institute for Sustainable Agriculture
220 Harmony Lane
Garberville, CA 95542
info@imisa.org
(877) 936-9663
www.imisa.org

Kitchen Gardeners International
7 Flintlock Drive
Scarborough, ME 04074
info@kitchengardeners.org
(207) 883-6773
www.kitchengardeners.org

Maine Organic Farmers and Gardeners Association
P.O. Box 170
Unity, ME 04988
mofga@mofga.org
(207) 568-4142
www.mofga.org

Missouri Organic Association
Rick Hopkins
P.O. Box 190
Marionville MO 65705-0190
rdhopkins@americanpasturage.com
(417) 258-2394
www.missouriorganic.org

Nanaimo Community Gardens Society
271 Pine St.
Nanaimo BC V9R 2B7
Canada
nanaimogardens@uniserve.com
(250) 753-9393
communitygardens.tripod.com/nanaimo

Northeast Organic Farming Association
Bill Duesing
Box 135
Stevenson, CT 06491
(203) 888-5146
bduesing@cs.com
www.ctnofa.org

The Rodale Institute Experimental Farm
611 Siegfriedale Rd.
Kutztown, PA 19530-9749
info@rodaleinst.org
(610) 683-1400
www.rodaleinstitute.org

Seattle Tilth Association
4649 Sunnyside Avenue
North, #1
Seattle, WA 98103-6900
tilth@seattletilth.org
(206) 633-0451
www.seattletilth.org

Tsaile Garden Club
P. O. Box 727
Faculty Hogan C-4
Tsaile, AZ 86556-0727
nwpark@yahoo.com
(520) 724-3445

Tucson Organic Gardeners
P.O. Box 27763
Tucson, AZ 85726
tucsonorganicgardeners@hotmail.com
(520) 670-9158
iwhome.com/nonprofits/TOG

Sources

Ackerman, Diane. *The Moon By Whale Light: And Other Adventures Among Bats, Penguins, Crocodilians, and Whales.* New York: Random House, 1991.

Appelhof, Mary. *Worms Eat My Garbage: How to Set Up and Maintain a Worm Composting System.* Kalamazoo, MI: Flower Press, 1997.

Ashworth, Suzanne. *Seed to Seed: Seed Saving Techniques for the Vegetable Gardener.* Decorah, Iowa: Seed Saver Publications, 1991.

Assadourian, Erik. "Cultivating the Butterfly Effect." *World Watch Magazine.* World Watch Institute, January/February 2003.

Ausubel, Kenny. *Restoring the Earth: Visionary Solutions from the Bioneers.* Tiburon, California: H. J. Kramer, 1997.

———. *Seeds of Change: The Living Treasure.* New York: Harper Collins, 1994.

Barrette, Elizabeth. "Greenwitch: An Invocation to Airmid." *Circle Network News.* Number 60, Summer 1996.

Bartholomew, Mel. *Square Foot Gardening: A New Way to Garden in Less Space with Less Work.* New York: Rodale Books, 2005.

Been, Vicki. "The Effect of Community Gardens on Neighboring Property Values." NYU Law and Economics Research Paper No. 06-09. Abstract online at Social Science Research Network, ssrn.com/abstract=889113. Accessed September 20, 2006.

Caddy, Eileen. *The Spirit of Findhorn.* New York: Harper and Row, 1976.

Carr-Gomm, Philip and Stephanie. *The Druid Animal Oracle.* New York: Simon and Schuster, 1994.

Clark, Rulon W. "Social Lives of Rattlesnakes." *Natural History.* March 2005, 37–42.

Cleeton, James. "Organic foods in relation to nutrition and health key facts." 11 July 2004. This factsheet is a summary of an article published in Coronary and Diabetic Care in the UK 2004 by the Association of Primary Care Groups and Trusts (UK). www.organicconsumers.org/organic/health-benefits.cfm, accessed December 8, 2005.

Coleman, Eliot. *Four-Season Harvest: Organic Vegetables from Your Home Garden All Year Long.* White River Junction, VT: Chelsea Green Publishing, 1999.

Conway, D. J. *Magick of the Gods and Goddesses: Invoking the Power of the Ancient Gods.* Berkeley: The Crossing Press, 2003.

Cunningham, Scott. *Cunningham's Encyclopedia of Magical Herbs.* St. Paul: Llewellyn, 2003.

Curott, Phyllis. *Witchcrafting: A Spiritual Guide to Making Magic.* New York: Broadway Books, 2001.

Damon, Betsy, and Anne Mavor. "The Living Water Garden." *Whole Earth,* Spring 2000, (100), 20–24.

"Dorothy MacLean: A Spirit in the Smokies Interview." *Spirit in the Smokies.* May 25, 1999. Electronic file at www.spiritinthesmokies.com/interviews/dorothym.html, accessed on June 10, 2005.

Erlich, Gretel. Quoted in Ellen Dugan, *Garden Witchery: Magic from the Ground Up.* St. Paul, Llewellyn, 2003.

Fortune, Dion. "The Charge of the Goddess." *Rebirth of Witchcraft.* Blaine, WA: Phoenix Publishing, 1989.

Fox, Matthew. *Creativity: Where the Divine and Human Meet.* Tarcher/Putnam, 2002.

———. *A Spirituality Named Compassion.* San Francisco: Harper & Row, 1979.

Franklin, Anna. *Lammas: Celebrating the Fruit of the First Harvest.* St. Paul: Llewellyn, 2001.

———. *Midsummer: Magical Celebrations of the Summer Solstice.* St. Paul: Llewellyn, 2003.

Gardner, Gary, and Brian Halweil. "Overfed and Underfed: The Global Epidemic of Malnutrition." *Worldwatch Paper 150.* March 2000.

"Glad for the Wild Garden." Interview with Rosemary Gladstar. *Herbal Voices,* 1999. Electronic document, www. awakenedwoman. com/rosemary__gladstar. htm, accessed June 10, 2005.

Gladstar, Rosemary. *Rosemary Gladstar's Family Herbal: A Guide to Living Life with Energy, Health, and Vitality.* North Adams, Massachusetts: Storey Books, 2001.

Gladstar, Rosemary and Pamela Hirsch. *Planting the Future.* Rochester, Vermont: Healing Arts Press, 2000.

"Globetrotting Food Will Travel Farther Than Ever This Thanksgiving." Worldwatch Institute, press release, November 21 2002. Retrieved March 25, 2005, at www.worldwatch.org/press/news/2002/11/21/.

Hackman, R. M., and E. L. Wagner. "The Senior Gardening and Nutrition Project: Development and Transport of a Dietary Behavior Change and Health Promotion Program." *Journal of Nutrition Education* (Nov/Dec 1990, v. 22 [6]), 262–270.

Hafiz. *The Gift.* Trans. By Daniel Ladinsky. New York: Penguin Compass, 1999.

Halweil, Brian. "Home Grown: The Case for Local Food in a Global Market." *Worldwatch Paper 163,* November 2002.

Haynes, Roslynn. "Sky and Telescope." September 1997,

72–75. Retrieved online on February 8, 2006, from solar-center.stanford.edu/folklore/aborigine.html.

Heaton, Shane. *Organic Farming, Food Quality, and Human Health: A Review of the Evidence.* Bristol: Soil Association, 2001 (PDF online at soilassociation.org.)

Hemenway, Toby. *Gaia's Garden: A Guide to Home-Scale Permaculture.* White River Junction, VT: Chelsea Green, 2000.

Hinrichsen, Don. "A Human Thirst." *World Watch Magazine.* World Watch Institute, January/February 2003.

Hoffman, David. *New Holistic Herbal.* New York: Barnes & Noble Books, 1995.

Ingerman, Sandra. *Medicine for the Earth.* New York: Three Rivers Press, 2001.

iVillage Garden Web. Gardening Organizations Directory. 2006. dir.gardenweb.com/directory/nph-ind.cgi

Jeavons, John. *How to Grow More Vegetables.* Berkeley: Ten Speed Press, 1979.

Jensen, Derrick. *A Language Older than Words.* White River Junction, Vermont: Chelsea Green, 2004.

Kilman, Scott. "U.S. Food Imports Now Exceed Exports." *The Agribusiness Examiner.* November 10, 2004. Issue #379.

Kohlleppel, T.; S. Jacob, and J. C. Bradley. "A Walk Through The Garden: Can a Visit to a Botanic Garden Reduce Stress?" *HortTechnology* (July/Sept 2002, v. 12 [3]), 489–492.

Kourik, Robert. *Drip Irrigation for Every Landscape and All Climates: Helping Your Garden Flourish, While Conserving Water!* Metamorphic Press, 1993.

Lee, Shannon, et al. Solar Folklore. Stanford Solar Center website. solar-center.stanford.

edu/folklore/folklore.html, accessed February 6, 2006.

Leiss, J. K., and D. A. Savitz. "Home Pesticide Use and Childhood Cancer: A Case-Control Study." *American Journal of Public Health.* New York, N.Y. (Feb 1995, v. 85 [2]), 249–252.

MacLean, Dorothy. *To Hear the Angels Sing: An Odyssey of Co-Creation with the Devic Kingdom.* Herndon, VA: Lidisfarne Books, 1994.

Marks, William A. *The Holy Order of Water: Healing Earth's Waters and Ourselves.* Great Barrington, MA: Bell Pond Books, 2001.

McFarland, Phoenix. *The Complete Book of Magical Names.* St. Paul: Llewellyn, 1999.

Monaghan, Patricia. *The New Book of Goddesses and Heroines.* St. Paul: Llewellyn, 1997.

Morrison, Dorothy. *Yule: A Celebration of Light and Warmth.* St. Paul: Llewellyn, 2000.

Morse, Roger A., and Nicholas W. Calderone. "The Value of Honey Bees as Pollinators of U.S. Crops in 2000." *Bee Culture Magazine.* March 2000.

Moskin, Julia. "Women Find Their Place in the Field." *The New York Times,* June 1, 2005.

Murray, Elizabeth. *Cultivating Sacred Spaces.* Petaluma, CA: Pomegranate Publications, 1998.

Muten, Burleigh. *Goddesses: A World of Myth and Magic.* Cambridge, MA: Barefoot Books, 2003.

Northup, Christiane, MD. *Women's Bodies, Women's Wisdom: Creating Physical and Emotional Health and Healing.* New York: Bantam, 1998.

"Pesticide Residues from Non-Organic Foods Building Up in Our Bodies." Pesticide Action Network. May 11, 2004. www.organicconsumers.

org/foodsafety/residues 052404.cfm, accessed December 8, 2005.

Pickrell, John. "Bats Boom on Organic Farms, Study Says." *National Geographic News.* February 2, 2004. Retrieved March 30, 2005, at news.national geographic.com/ news/2004/02/0202__ 040202__bats.html.

Pollan, Michael. *The Omnivore's Dilemma: A Natural History of Four Meals.* New York: Penguin Press, 2006.

Postel, Sandra, and Brian Richter. *Rivers for Life: Managing Water for People and Nature.* Washington, D.C.: Island Press, 2003.

Riofrio, Marianne, and E. C. Wittmeyer. "Improving Soils for Vegetable Gardening." Ohio State University Extension Fact Sheet HYG-1602-92. ohioline.osu.edu/ hyg-fact/1000/1602.html, accessed March 13, 2005.

Sams, Jamie, and David Carson. *Medicine Cards: The Discovery of Power Through the Ways of Animals.* Santa Fe: Bear & Co, 1988.

Schwenk, Theodor. *Sensitive Chaos: The Creation of Flowing Forms in Water and Air.* London: Rudolf Steiner Press, 1990.

Shapiro, Howard-Yana, and John Harrisson. *Gardening for the Future of the Earth.* New York: Bantam Books, 2000.

Smillie, Joseph, and Grace Gershuny. *The Soul of Soil: A Soil-Building Guide for Master Gardeners and Farmers.* White River Junction, VT: Chelsea Green, 1999.

Starhawk. *The Earth Path: Grounding Your Spirit in the Rhythms of Nature.* New York: HarperSan-Francisco, 2004.

———. *The Fifth Sacred Thing.* New York: Bantam, 1994.

———. *The Spiral Dance: A Rebirth of the Ancient Religion of the Goddess: 20th Anniversary Edition.* New York: HarperSanFrancisco, 1999.

———. *Webs of Power: Notes from the Global Uprising.* Gabriola Island, B.C.: New Society Publishers, 2002.

Stewart, Amy. *The Earth Moved: On the Remarkable Achievement of Earthworms.* Chapel Hill, NC: Algonquin, 2005

Sullivan, Dan. "Organic Gardens Help Fight Global Warming." *Organic Gardening.* Jan/Feb 2004, 51(1).

Summers, Adam. "How Trees Get High." *Natural History.* March 2005. P. 35.

Tielmans, E., R. van Kooij, ER te Velde, A. Burdof, and D. Heederik. "Pesticide Exposure and Decreased Fertilization Rates In Vitro." *Lancet,* August 7, 1999, 484–485.

Tuxill, John. "Nature's Cornucopia: Our Stake in Plant Diversity." *Worldwatch Paper 148.* World Watch Institute, September 1998.

Walker, Barbara. *The Woman's Encyclopedia of Myths and Secrets.* New York: Harper SanFrancisco, 1983.

Weed, Susun. *Healing Wise.* Woodstock, NY: Ash Tree Publishing, 1989.

Winning, Rebecca. "From the Roots: Gardeners Cultivate Food Diversity, Savor Culture." *The Underground News* (vol. 10, no. 3). Spring 2005, p. 1.

Wright, Machaelle Small. *Co-Creative Science: A Revolution in Science Providing Real Solutions for Today's Health & Environment.* Jefferston, Virginia: Perelandra, 1997.

Wyant, Ty. "Gardening Views You Can Use: Q & A with Rob Proctor." *Boulder County Home & Garden Magazine.* Spring 2004. Boulder, CO: Brock Publishing Corp.

Index

Free Magazine

Read unique articles by Llewellyn authors, recommendations by experts, and information on new releases. To receive a **free** copy of Llewellyn's consumer magazine, *New Worlds of Mind & Spirit,* simply call 1-877-NEW-WRLD or visit our website at www.llewellyn.com and click on *New Worlds.*

Llewellyn Ordering Information

Order Online:

Visit our website at www.llewellyn.com, select your books, and order them on our secure server.

Order by Phone:

- Call toll-free within the U.S. at 1-877-NEW-WRLD (1-877-639-9753). Call toll-free within Canada at 1-866-NEW-WRLD (1-866-639-9753)
- We accept VISA, MasterCard, and American Express

Order by Mail:

Send the full price of your order (MN residents add 6.5% sales tax) in U.S. funds, plus postage & handling to:

Llewellyn Worldwide
2143 Wooddale Drive, Dept. 0-7387-1146-2
Woodbury, MN 55125-2989, U.S.A.

Postage & Handling:

Standard (U.S., Mexico, & Canada). If your order is:
$24.99 and under, add $3.00
$25.00 and over, FREE STANDARD SHIPPING

AK, HI, PR: $15.00 for one book plus $1.00 for each additional book.

International Orders (airmail only):
$16.00 for one book plus $3.00 for each additional book

Orders are processed within 2 business days.
Please allow for normal shipping time. Postage and handling rates subject to change.

Garden Witchery: Magick from the Ground Up

Ellen Dugan

Includes a Gardening Journal!

How does your magickal garden grow? *Garden Witchery* is more than belladonna and wolfsbane. It's about making your own enchanted backyard with the trees, flowers, and plants found growing around you. It's about creating your own flower fascinations and spells, and it's full of common-sense information about cold hardiness zones, soil requirements, and a realistic listing of accessible magickal plants.

There may be other books on magickal gardening, but none have practical gardening advice, magickal correspondences, flower folklore, moon gardening, faerie magick, advanced witchcraft, and humorous personal anecdotes all rolled into one volume.

• • •

0-7387-0318-4: 272 pp., 7½ x 7½, illus., $16.95

Cunningham's Encyclopedia of Magical Herbs

Scott Cunningham

Also Available in Spanish!

This is the most comprehensive source of herbal data for magical uses ever printed! Almost every one of the over four hundred herbs are illustrated, making this a great source for herb identification. For each herb you will also find magical properties, planetary rulerships, genders, associated deities, folk and Latin names, and much more.

To make this book even easier to use, it contains a folk name cross-reference, and all of the herbs are fully indexed. There is also a large annotated bibliography, and a list of mail-order suppliers so you can find the books and herbs you need.

Like all of Cunningham's books, this one does not require you to use complicated rituals or expensive magical paraphernalia. Instead, it shares with you the intrinsic powers of the herbs. Thus, you will be able to discover which herbs, by their very nature, can be used for luck, love, success, money, divination, astral projection, safety, psychic self-defense, and much more.

• • •

0-875422-9: 336 pp., 6 x 9, illus., $14.95

. . . .

To Write to the Author

If you wish to contact the author or would like more information about this book, please write to the author in care of Llewellyn Worldwide and we will forward your request. Both the author and publisher appreciate hearing from you and learning of your enjoyment of this book and how it has helped you. Llewellyn Worldwide cannot guarantee that every letter written to the author can be answered, but all will be forwarded. Please write to:

Clea Danaan
℅ Llewellyn Worldwide
2143 Wooddale Drive,
Dept. 0-7387-1146-2
Woodbury, MN
55125-2989, U.S.A.

Please enclose a self-addressed stamped envelope for reply or $1.00 to cover costs. If outside U.S.A., enclose international postal reply coupon.

SACRED LAND is printed on recycled, 50% post-consumer waste 55# cream offset paper using Vendetta type and ornaments with the occasional Black Chancery initial cap. Illustrations are gratefully acknowledged from *Old-Fashioned Floral Designs CD-ROM and Book*